Helen M. Pernin

Pernin's Practical Reporter

A Complete Guide to Verbatim Reporting

Helen M. Pernin

Pernin's Practical Reporter
A Complete Guide to Verbatim Reporting

ISBN/EAN: 9783337399931

Printed in Europe, USA, Canada, Australia, Japan

Cover: Foto ©Lupo / pixelio.de

More available books at **www.hansebooks.com**

Pernin's

Practical Reporter.

A COMPLETE GUIDE

TO

Verbatim Reporting.

COMPILED AND PUBLISHED BY

H. M. PERNIN.

DETROIT, MICH.:
O. S. GULLEY PRINTING HOUSE, 19, 14 AND 16 LARNED STREET EAST.
1882.

ENTERED ACCORDING TO ACT OF CONGRESS, MAY, 1882, BY
H. M. PERNIN,
IN THE OFFICE OF THE LIBRARIAN OF CONGRESS,
WASHINGTON, D. C.

PREFACE.

On commencing the study of the Reporting Style contained in the present volume, the short-hand student must necessarily be familiar with the principles of the Corresponding Course, which precedes this, and also be able to write *correctly* with it. After correctness is attained, it is not essential that the student should linger upon it, although the greater ease with which he can write in it will assist him much in using the contracted style with rapidity.

The modes of contraction presented in the present volume are formed, for the most part, from the actual experience of the author, both as reporter and teacher of the art. In this, as well as in the preceding course, the exercises are graded. A small portion only of the contractions are given in each lesson, so that even the youngest learner will not become puzzled or discouraged by attempting to memorize too many rules or illustrations, before putting each rule or illustration into practical use. In this method the Reading Exercises are placed immediately after the illustrations, so that the application may be seen at once in them, and transferred to actual practice in the Writing Exercises which follow.

The present mode of contraction is not based, as in other methods, upon arbitrary word signs, but upon the application of eight simple rules depending upon the proximity or distance from it of the word following the contracted one.

But for very small and frequently recurring words, many of which are found in nearly every article that is written, the eye becomes so accustomed to the form that they may be written in the same manner as if they were contracted by rule, and yet be readily recognized without the next word being placed in position. The alphabetic and miniature word-signs, found in the annexed table, are adopted into the Reading Exercises from the beginning, and the learner should practice writing the table a number of times, until he is perfectly familiar with its contents, and can write them readily and recognize them at a glance in the Reading Exercises. Later on, a more extended list is given. but as the entire number is not more than a couple of hundred, the mind will not be greatly taxed in remembering them.

On the pages opposite the Reading Exercises will be found the same matter in print in the Writing Exercises. but the student should not refer to them except in cases where it is absolutely necessary. Before writing he should peruse the Reading Exercise, carefully, a number of times until he becomes familiar with it, and he will then be able to translate the opposite page of print very readily into short-hand again. By taking up the forms of contraction a little at a time, the learner will have no difficulty in readily applying them; and when the last chapter has been reached he will find that he has the contractions fully at his command without any effort at memorizing, and can apply them without hesitation. A large number of Reading and Writing Exercises is given for the purpose of making the short-hand student thoroughly familiar with his work by the time he has gone through the pages of the present volume.

ADVICE TO STUDENTS ON TAKING UP THE REPORTING STYLE.

In the first place, write over the contents of the table of alphabetic word-signs a number of times, until perfectly familiar with their forms, and then apply them in all the following writing exercises.

Study each of the illustrations so thoroughly that it will not be necessary to refer to them on subsequent occasions. When they are fully impressed upon the mind, go over the Reading Exercise that follows, and carefully note their application, meantime covering the Writing Exercise so that the eye will not rest upon it; only referring to it in difficult cases. When this has been done, translate the Reading Exercise into long-hand, and then compare your manuscript with the Writing Exercise in book, with which it should agree. If correct, close the book, and translate your long-hand matter into short-hand. This done, again refer to the book, and see if it agrees with the short-hand matter in Reading Exercise. In class, the students may exchange and read each other's manuscript, and the teacher may then compare them with original in book.

Do not be confined to the exercises given in the "Reporter," but write articles from newspapers, magazines, etc. *Read everything that you write.* This is of essential importance. It is worse than useless to spend your time in learning to *write* short-hand unless you are able to read it readily.

If possible, engage some one to read aloud to you while practicing. This plan will save much time, and is much more satisfactory than being obliged to continually refer to the article being copied. It will also accustom one to dictation, and does away with that feeling of nervousness natural to those beginning practical work without having this advantage.

Practice regularly, two hours per day if possible; much more is accomplished in two months with even half that amount of practice than in six months of spasmodic exertions. Theory will never make a reporter; the hand, as well as the head, has its own share of work to perform, and in order to be a successful short-hand writer, both must work together.

Every possible opportunity should be embraced for

putting your knowledge of the art into practical use. Always carry a small note-book and pencil, and on every occasion that presents itself, jot down conversations, sermons, lectures and so on, or as much of them as you can. Do not be discouraged if the speaker gets ahead of you. When you begin a sentence, always complete it. You are yet only a student, not an expert, and cannot expect to take the whole discourse verbatim. It will be much more satisfactory when you come to translate your notes, to find that you have taken a few complete sentences, than pages of matter that you can make no sense of.

Little by little the required speed will come. Never allow yourselves to be discouraged. *You* can surely accomplish what so many have accomplished before you, and the feat is not so very difficult. What other branch of learning could you acquire in the few months' time that this demands? There is no royal road to learning of any kind, and short-hand is no exception. "Practice" must be the motto of him who desires to become a reporter. Do not let this practice cease when your writing is rapid enough for office work. Fit yourself for any department of the work. By this method there is no more study required for one branch than another, but the student must keep up his practice until he acquires rapidity enough for newspaper, court reporting, etc. Then, if an opening occurs, he will be competent to fill it, provided his general education is what the position demands. The student as he advances may contract his writing by rule still shorter than that contained in the Reading Exercises in the book, as these exercises are only intended for the learner, and not for the expert.

PHONOGRAPHIC ALPHABET.

CONSONANTS.

`|`	p	*p*ray	`\`	f	*f*at	`⌣`	s, z.	*s*ee, *z*ee.
`|`	b	*b*ray	`\`	v	*v*at	`⌒`	sh, zh,	*sh*e, a*z*ure.
`/`	k	*k*ey	`/`	l	*l*aw	`⌒`	je, ch,	*j*aw, *ch*aw.
`/`	g	*g*o	`/`	r	*r*aw	`)`	m,	*m*e.
`—`	t	*t*o	`.`	h	*h*e	`)`	n,	*n*o.
`—`	d	*d*o	`⊥`	th	*th*e	`)`	ng,	si*ng*.

VOWELS.

○	ah	*a*t	`⌣`	uh	*u*p
○	au	*a*ll	`⌒`	ā	*a*te
○	ow	*ow*l	`⊂`	ē	*ea*t
○	o	*o*ld	`⌒`	ĕ, ĭ	b*e*t, b*i*t
`(`	oo	h*oo*k			

NASAL COMBINATIONS.

`⌐`	an	p*an*.
`\`	en, in,	p*en*.
`⌒`	on, un,	up*on*.

(Before *p* and *b*, am, em, im, om, um, take the same form respectively as the above.)

a*m*ple, e*m*pire h*um*ble

LESSON I.

ALPHABETIC WORD-SIGNS.   **SIGNS FOR FAMILIAR WORDS.**

o·	ah, at.		before.
o	awe, all.		after.
ɞ	our, out.		afterwards.
·ꙩ	how.		from.
o	oh, owe, owing.		most.
(	who.		never.
⌣	of.		ever.
⌢	aye.		every.
⌣	he.		above.
ɔ	you.		perhaps.
)	we.		almost.
∕	I.		number.
⌐	an.		what.
⌐	one.		that.
⌣	when.	=	to the.
ǀ	put.		behind.
ǀ	but.		beyond.
∕	could, quite.		upon.
∕	good, go.		without.
—	the, (*to*, when joined to next word).		also.
——	and, (*do*, when joined to next word).		about.
⟍	for.	(	whom.
⟍	very.		woman.
⟋	less.		because.
⟋	railway, sign of repetition.		whoever.
⌣	so, such.		whatever.
⌒	should, sure.		whenever.
⌒	judge, church, just.		forever.
⟨	more, much.	Z	together.
⟩	no, not.		thou.
⟩	knowing, known		now.

READING AND WRITING EXERCISE I.

1. No man can safely speak but he who loves silence.

2. Of all the sisters of Love, the most charming is Pity.

3. No one is placed on earth to do nothing.

4. Everyone must find out for himself the key to the riddle of life.

5. People seldom improve when they have no other model but themselves to copy after.

6. Make up your minds to do a thing and you will do it.

7. The sun set behind us, but before us was the sea.

8. Be sure you are right—then go ahead.

9. Before all and above all, to thine own self be true.

10. "Whatever you do, do it well," is a very good motto.

11. It is much more easy to preach than to practice.

12 How much of each of our lives is lost beyond recall!

13 You all did love him once, not without cause. What
cause withholds you now to mourn for him?

14 Put not your trust in money, but put your money in trust.

15 Look at those to whom you speak; never at those of
whom you speak.

16 Yesterday is as to-morrow in the forever.

17 Leisure is too beautiful a garment for every-day wear.

18 The good judge was kind and just to all offenders.

19 This poor woman is the one of whom I spoke to you.

20 We will go there together, before the flowers have faded.

21 What more could anyone have done upon that occasion?

22 It is now quite dark at five o'clock in the afternoon.

23 Waste neither time nor money, but make the best
use of both.

SUPPRESSION OF WORDS.

In reporting a lecture, or writing from dictation, such words as *a, an, the, and, of, at, to, upon, by, from,* and others of a similar nature, may be frequently omitted when the sense of the sentence will oblige them to be restored. The reporter must, however, rely on his own judgment as to the extent these omissions may be carried. Where his work is of such a particular nature that the substitution of *a* for *the* might give a different meaning to the text, it would be safer in such cases to write every word, but a little license in this respect may be sometimes taken with advantage.

JOINING OF WORDS.

The words *to, do* and *so* may be joined to the words that follow them by dropping the (sign, which cannot always be readily combined in a word, and adding the - to the following word, thus: *to-see,* *to-say,* *to-go* or still shorter, by using the word sign / for *go* *To-do-so* may be written ; *to-do-him* ; *so-far* .

This principle of joining simple words together may be employed wherever it does not interfere with clearness in reading the combinations. Parts of the verb may be nearly always joined; thus: *to-be* ' ; *to-have-been* ; *could-have-been* ; and when the subject is a pronoun, it may also be added, as: *it-may-be* ; *he-could* ; *you-will* ; *we-were* . On, in and *of* may also be joined to the words following, as *on-the* , *in-the* , *in-which* , *on-their* , *of-them* *of-it* .

READING EXERCISE II.

(shorthand content)

WRITING EXERCISE II.

I once had a dream, and yet it-was-not *all* a dream, in-which it seemed to-me *that* I set *out upon* a long journey through a dark valley, which was called "The Valley of Tears."

The valley had this name *because* those who-were traveling through it, met with many sorrowful trials on-their way, and *most* of-them left it in *very* great pain and anguish. It-was full *of-all* manner *of* people, *of-all* ages and colors and conditions, yet *all* were traveling in-the same direction; or, rather, although they were taking many different paths, these *all* led *to-the* same common end.

I noticed, *also, that* these people, though differing *so-much* in complexion, ages, tempers, were *all* alike in *one* respect—each had a burden on-his back, which he-was compelled to-carry through the toil and heat *of*-the day, until he-should arrive at his journey's end.

It-would-have-been *very* hard *for*-the poor pilgrims to-bear up under the toils *of-such* a journey, had-*not* the Lord *of*-the valley, *out-of* compassion *for*-them, provided, among other things, the following means *for* their relief: In-their full view, over the entrance to-the valley, He-had written in great letters *of*-gold, "Bear ye *one* another's burdens."

NOTE.—Words connected by hyphens are to be written together without raising the pen, and italicized words according to the table of word-signs.

REVIEW OF LESSON FIRST.

Name and write the Alphabetic Word-signs.

How is *ow* written? Write *you* in contracted form. Write *we*. How are *to, do* and *so* written when joined to the words that follow them? Write the table of familiar word signs. Why are these words formed into signs? What words may be sometimes omitted, and when? How are *on* and *in* written when they are prepositions? Write *an*. In what direction is the combination *an* written in a word? *En* or *in*? *On* or *un*? Write short *e* or *i* so as to distinguish it from long *e*.

LESSON II.

SUPPRESSION OF REPEATED WORDS AND PHRASES.

When a word or phrase is repeated in the same sentence, and sufficiently close to the first affirmation so as not to be misunderstood in reading, the repetition may be suppressed and the *r* sign / substituted in the place the repeated word or phrase would occupy, if written in full; thus: A place for *everything* and *everything* in its place, may be written,

In cases where a question is asked, and a negative reply given embodying the words of the question, the negative may be indicated by the *n* sign) followed by the sign of repetition; thus— *You will remember the time? No, you will not remember it, for you were too young*—may be written

PUNCTUATION.

The dot being used for other purposes in shorthand; the

Period is indicated by .... ×

Dash —— "   " .... ——

Wonder   "   " .... ∕

Grief   "   " .... ∕

Laughter   "   " ....)

The interrogation and exclamation points, the comma, semicolon, colon and quotation marks are similar to those in ordinary writing. Proper names, when written in short-hand are indicated by a single short waved line beneath, and should not be abbreviated except when repeated more than once.

READING AND WRITING EXERCISE III.
ON REPETITIONS.

If there-be one man before me who honestly and contentedly believes that, on-the whole, he is doing that work to-which his powers are best adapted, I wish to-congratulate him. My friend, I care not whether your hand be hard or soft; *I care not whether you have seen the inside of-a college or the outside*—whether your work be that of-the head or *of the* hand—whether the world accounts you noble or ignoble; if you-have found your place you-are a happy man. Let no ambition ever tempt you away from it by so much as a questioning thought. I say, if *you-have found your place*—no matter where or what it-is—you are a happy man. I give you joy of your good fortune: for if you-do-the work of that place well, and draw from it all that it-can-give you of merriment, and discipline, and development, you-are or you-will become a man filled up, made after God's pattern, the noblest product of the world—a self-made man.

REVIEW OF LESSON SECOND.

How may a repeated word or phrase be indicated? When the repetition is in the negative, how is it indicated? How are the Punctuation Marks represented in short-hand? How are proper names indicated? When should they be abbreviated and when not?

LESSON III.
OMISSION OF CONSONANTS.

The learner may have observed that, in common pronunciation, certain consonants are heard very indistinctly, and as there is no difficulty in understanding the speaker under such circumstances, so, by dropping these indistinct consonant sounds in short-hand, something will be gained in rapid execution, and the writing will still remain sufficiently legible. In ordinary conversation, *of* has the sound of *uh;* thus: *A lump of coal.* Here and in similar instances *of* sounds like *uh,* and the sign of *uh*, as given in the table of alphabetic word-signs, may be substituted for it, either where it stands alone in a sentence or where it is used in a combination. This sound, which is also the short sound of *u*, may be used for long *u* in cases where the latter does not unite readily with the sign following it; or the sign may be omitted and a dot placed immediately under the place it would occupy if written; thus: *beauty* ⌐ *pure* ⌐. This is according to a rule given further on in the book, but may be adopted with advantage here.

T may be omitted after *k*, as: *facts*   *extract*
T   "   "   "   *n*, as: *constantly*   *silent*
T   "   "   "   *s*, as: *must*   *past*
T   "   "   "   *p*, as: *abrupt*   *prompt*
D   "   "   "   *n*, as: *kindly*   *mindful*
D   "   "   before *m*, as: *admirer*   *admit*
D   "   "   " *v* and *f*, as: *advise* *dreadful*
R   "   "   "   *gh*, as: *charge*   *margin*
R   "   "   " *m* and *s*, as: *former* *scarcely*
R   "   "   " *f* and *v*, as: *therefore* *preserve*
N   "   "   " *gh, gth*, as: *change*   *strength*
K   "   "   "   *s*, as: *success*   *expect*

Where *t* and *d* follow each other in the same word, the first of the two signs may be omitted; as: *Spendthrift*. When a word follows another whose initial sign is similar to the final sign of the preceding one, or when one of the signs is *t* — and the other *d* — the final sign may be dropped, and the two words joined, as: *A silk cloak* · *short time* · *great deal*.

READING EXERCISE IV.
ON THE OMISSION OF CONSONANTS.

WRITING EXERCISE IV.
ON THE OMISSION OF CONSONANTS.

1 Experience is the extract of suffering.
2 I am not unmindful of the favors you have bestowed upon me.
3 My friend intends leaving for Europe next week.
4 The order for the work was promptly filled according to agreement.
5 Charles, on hearing the sad news, abruptly left the apartment.
6 We do-not need precepts so-much-as patterns.
7 It-must-be done; there-is no help for it.
8 The judge asked the advocate if he believed the prisoner guilty.
9 Man looketh on-the face, but God seeth into-the heart.
10 All is vanity except to-love God and to-serve Him only.
11 Our grand business is-not to-see what lies dimly at a distance but to-do what lies clearly at hand.
12 Matters are indeed a great-deal worse than I supposed.
13 This grand reception, given so shortly after his father's death, was in very bad-taste.
14 Praise at the right-time and in-the right place is a wonderful helper.
15 Youth changes its tastes by the warmth of its blood; age retains its taste by the force of habit.
16 We understand death for the first-time when he puts his hand on one that we love.
17 It is easier to be wise for others than to-be-so for one's self.
18 We are fearfully and wonderfully made.

REVIEW OF LESSON THIRD.

How is *of* sounded in ordinary pronunciation? Give an example. How may it be written in short-hand? What sign is sometimes substituted for long *u*? When it is omitted, what is used to indicate its suppression? When may *t* be suppressed? When *d*? When *r*? When *n*? When *t* and *d* follow each other in a word, how is it written? When one word ends in *t* or *d*, and the following word begins with *d* or *t*, what is done? When the initial sign of a word and the final sign of the word preceding it are similar, what is done?

LESSON IV.
SUPPRESSION OF SIMILAR CONSONANTS.

In writing words containing two vertical or two oblique consonant strokes, combinations such as *bab* or *rer*, take an awkward form; and in order to preserve the symmetry of the writing, and at the same time promote rapidity, the first consonant may be written in full and the second indicated by a sudden pressure of the pen or pencil upon the end of the first consonant; thus: *Barrier*   *babble*

Similar consonants traced in a horizontal direction may be abbreviated in the same manner with advantage; thus: *system   success   tetter* Tet and ted may be contracted by the foregoing rule without distinction, for were *catet* written instead of *cadet*, the general context of the sentence would be a sufficient guide to the correct word. When *t* is preceded by *d*, it follows the same rule; as: *debtor*   Should any instance occur, however, when by following this rule the reading would become obscure, the *t* and *d* signs should be written separately.

READING EXERCISE VI.

WRITING EXERCISE V.

Carrier, furrier, barrier, parallel, warrior, superior, inferior, courier, career, lily, filial, causes, misses, opposes, discusses, amazes, scissors, Cesar, teases, possesses, resists, sizes, losses, endorses, ceded, elected, mated, abated, deeded, faded, jaded, goaded, coated, braided, impeded, exceeded, kneaded, pleaded, meted, lighted, guided, benighted, righted, knighted, delighted, beaded, plated, laded, completed, babble, probable, people, pepper, goggle, cackle, bibber, bible.

ABBREVIATIONS IN FINAL *rl* and *lr*.

The contractions for final *rl* and *lr*, like those contained in the preceding exercise, are introduced for the purpose of dispensing with the awkward appearance which these two upward strokes present when written one after another. Final *r* may therefore be indicated by a slight upward tick inclining to the left; thus: *peddler* ⌣ , *teller* ⌣ and final *l* by a slight upward tick to the right; thus: *furl* ⌣ *moral* ⌣ . These ticks must be made by the lightest possible drop of the pen, very short, so as not to be confounded with *i*, and written in a straight, inclined direction, so as not to be mistaken for any of the Nasal Combinations. When a word terminates in *l* or *r* which contains a similar sign either at the beginning or in the middle of the word, the final *l* or *r* may also be indicated by the tick sign; thus: *latter* ⌣ *riddle* ⌣ If care is taken in the formation of the tick signs, they may also be introduced into words containing the upward strokes which do not terminate the word; as: *Curls* ⌣ *furls* ⌣ *carols.* ⌣ .

READING EXERCISE VI.

WRITING EXERCISE VI.

Barrel, whirl, carol, peddler, unfurl, curl, pearl, caller, teller, sterile, girl, laurel, oral, jailer, paler, railer, sailor, tailor, whaler, exhaler, staler, earl, churl, moral, sorrel, miller, letter, ladder, rather, ladle, cradle, braver.

READING EXERCISE VII.

WRITING EXERCISE VII.

1 The benighted and jaded traveler pleaded with the kind-hearted farmer to-remain over night to rest.

2 The poor sailor was delighted at being permitted to embark on-the whaler bound for the Arctic seas.

3 The bank teller was upbraided by his superior officer with having forfeited his bonds, and handed over to the jailer.

4 The babble of the brook sounded in the ear like distant music.

5 The letter carrier completed his daily rounds and proved a most efficient courier.

6 The dusty-coated miller filled the empty barrel with flour, and drew forth the thanks of the delighted girl who at once proceeded to have it kneaded into bread.

7 The rural peddler unrolled a bale of cloth, which he finally traded to the tailor for a beaded cloak.

8 The younger soldier was the braver of the two, for he unfurled the flag in the face of the enemy.

9 The pretty girl wore a costly pearl necklace, which afforded her much pleasure.

10 The daring deeds of the robber excited the people to vengeance, and they exceeded the limits of the law.

11 The table of the noble earl was laden with triple-plated silver.

12 A chronic state of rebellion causes many losses to the people, and distresses more than it benefits them.

13 The big dog Cesar both teases and amuses the little black kitten which is unable to resist his approaches.

REVIEW OF LESSON FOURTH.

How may the second of two similar consonants be indicated which occurs in the same word? How may vertical or oblique consonants be contracted? Give the contractions for final *lr*. Write the final *rl*. How may these signs be written, when they follow each other but are not terminal signs?

LESSON V.

CONTRACTED PREFIXES.

As a great majority of words commence with the prefixes given in the present lesson, a contracted form of writing them will be found to be of much assistance in acquiring speed for reporting.

PRO, PRE, PER. These may be classed among the most frequently recurring prefixes, and may be abbreviated with great advantage. *Pro* is represented by a light accent written from right to left and placed near the beginning of the sign following the omitted prefix; thus: *protect   proceed   problem*

Pre is represented by a short inclined dash written downwards from right to left through the beginning of the following sign; thus: *predict   preserve   prefix*

Per is represented by a similar dash written in the opposite direction; thus: *permit   perfect   perjurer*

CON, COUN, COM. These prefixes are all contracted by the same form, which consists of a light accent written in the opposite direction to that used to represent *pro;* thus: *connect   conceal   complain   commit   country*

DIS, DES, is represented by a short dash placed immediately *above* the beginning of the following sign, as: *discreet   dissolve   despair*

MIS, MES, is represented by a short dash placed immediately *below* the beginning of the following sign, as: *mistake   message   misconstrue*

READING EXERCISE VIII.

On the Contracted Prefixes PRO, PRE, PER, CON, COUN, COM, DIS, DES, MIS, MES.

WRITING EXERCISE VIII.

Probable, probate, problem, proceed, proclaim, produce, profess, profane, proffer, profound, profit, progress, project, prolific, prolong, propose, protect, protest, protract, provide, provoke.

Precaution, precede, precept, precious, precise, predict, prefer, prefix, prelate, prepare, premise, prepay, presage, prescribe, present, preside.

Perceive, perdition, perfect, perform, peril, period, perish, perjure, permit, perplex, persevere, pertain, pervert, perspire, personate, perspective.

Conceal, concede, conceit, concise, concrete, condense, condole, confide, conflict, conform, confront, congeal, consent, consist, console, common, combat, compel, comfort, commend, counsel, country, county, countenance.

Disable, disagree, disarm, disaster, disgrace, disciple, disclose, discount, discard, displace, descend, describe, desert, design, desire, despair, desolate, destine.

Mistake, misplace, misdeed, mishap, mistrust, misuse, misprint, miserable, message, Messiah.

ADDITIONAL PREFIXES.

In addition to the previous list of prefixes, there are a number of others which, although not of such common occurrence as the former class, yet are written frequently enough to admit of contraction:

SUB, SUP, SURP, may be written in a contracted form by a vertical line passing through the following sign at about one-third of its length above the sign; thus: *suppose*   *subject*   *subtract*   *supply*   . As the *r* before *p* is very indistinctly heard in ordinary pronunciation, it may be omitted and the same contraction used for *surp* as for *sup;* *surprise*   *surpass*   .

TRANS may be represented by a short vertical line passing through the following sign at equal distances above and below; thus: *transact*   *transmit*   *transform*

SUPER, SUPRE, may be represented by a vertical line intersecting the following sign at two-thirds of its length above it: *supersede*   *superfine*   *supreme*   .

EXTRA, EXTRE, EXTRI, may be represented by a horizontal dash written through the following sign at a distance of two-thirds its length to the left; thus: *extract*   *extravagant*   *extreme*   .

INTER, ENTER, INTRO, may be represented by a short horizontal dash intersecting the following sign at equal distances; thus: *interest*   *enterprise*   *introvert*   .

CONTRA, CONTRI, CONTRO, COUNTER, may be represented by a short horizontal dash written through the following sign at a distance of two-thirds of its length to the right; thus: *contract*   *control*   *counteract*   *contribute*

NOTE.—In cases where the sign following the contracted prefix is traced in a similar direction to it, it is allowable to give the prefix an inclined form, taking care, however, to observe its proper distance at either end.

READING EXERCISE IX.

On the Contracted Prefixes SUB, SUP, SURP, TRANS, SUPER, SUPRE, EXTRA, EXTRE, EXTRI, INTER, ENTER, INTRO, CONTRA, CONTRI, CONTRO, COUNTER.

WRITING EXERCISE IX.

Subject, subdeacon, subdue, subjoin, sublime, submit, submissive, subscribe, subside, subsist, substance, subtract, suburb, subvert, support, supplant, supply, supplicate, suppose, supreme, surprise, surpass, surplice.

Transact, transcend, transcribe, transfer, transform, transgress, transient, translate, transport, transplant, transpire, transport, transpose, transverse, transitory, transparent, transmute.

Superb, supercilious, superficial, superfine, superintend, superlative, supersede, supervene, supervise, suppress, supreme.

Extravagant, extraction, extradition, extraordinary, extreme, extremity, extricate, extract, extraneous.

Interest, intercept, intercede, intercourse, interdict, interfere, interior, interject, interlard, interlude, interpose, interpret, interrogate, interest, interview. Enterprise, entertain, entirely. Introduce, introvert, intrude.

Contradict, contraband, contract, contrary, contrast. Contrite, contribute, contrive. Control, controversy. Council, countenance, counteract, counterpart, counterfeit, countersign, counterbalance, country.

TABLE OF CONTRACTED PREFIXES.

PREFIXES.	SIGN.	EXAMPLE.	APL'N.
Pro,	,	Product,	
Per, pre,	\ /	Persist, predict,	
Con, coun, com,	`	Conceit, compel,	
Dis, des,	ō	Dissolve, desert,	
Mis, mes,	ȩ	Missive, Messiah,	
Sub, sup, surp,	ɸ	Submit, supper,	
Trans,	ɸ	Transaction,	
Super, supre,	ɸ	Superb, supreme,	
Extra, extre, extri,	—•—	Extract, extreme,	
Inter, enter, intro,	—•—	Interest, intercede,	
Contra, contri, contro, counter	—•—	Contrary, control,	

DOUBLE PREFIXES.

Precon,		Preconceive,	
Unpre,		Unprepared,	
Discon,		Disconnect,	
Indis,		Indisposed,	
Miscon,		Misconduct,	
Uncon,		Uncontrollable,	
Recom, recon,		Recommend, reconcile,	
Irrecon,		Irreconcilement,	
Accom, accoun,		Accomplish, accountable,	

IRREGULAR PREFIXES.

For, fore,		Forbid, foretell,	
Self,		Selfish, self-control,	
Just,		Justify,	
Circum,		Circumflex,	
Retro, retri,		Retrograde, retribution,	
Repre,		Represent,	

Above and *over* are represented by a da**sh** above the word or sign following, as: *above the* — ; *overthrow* ; and *under* and *below* by a dash beneath; thus: *understand* ; *below him* ×

READING EXERCISE X.

[Page of shorthand notation]

WRITING EXERCISE X.

ON CONTRACTED PREFIXES.

1 *Mis*fortune has few riddles for him who believes that the sole *des*ign of *Pro*vidence is the *per*fecting of mankind.

2 If you cannot bring your *con*dition to your mind, bring your mind to your *con*dition.

3 The *mes*sage was left at three o'clock, and has *pro*bably been *trans*mitted some hours since.

4 The *super*ior fitness of the new *pro*prietors was fully proven at their recent *superb enter*tainment.

5 A number of *prominent* citizens *inter*ested themselves in the matter, and its *pro*gress was in a great *measure* due to their *pro*mptness.

6 The *des*titute orphan was *dis*consolate at the loss of his *pro*tector.

7 On their return, the *com*pany *dis*banded and were *dis*missed from the service.

8 That *mis*guided individual has effected much *mis*chief through his *con*stant *mis*representations.

9 The *ex*treme cold of a northern winter chilled the *trans*planted flower.

10 The *com*plainant *per*sisted in *inter*rupting the *coun*sel and *contra*dicting his statements. Owing to these unlooked-for *circum*stances, the judge did not feel *jus*tified in *recom*mending the prisoner to mercy.

11 The *pro*digal son was *for*given for his *extra*vagance and *mis*conduct, and a *recon*ciliation effected between him and his father.

REVIEW OF LESSON FIFTH.

What prefixes occur the most frequently? How may *pro* and *con* be contracted? What prefixes are contracted by a slanting line written through the following sign? What by a vertical line? State the exception to this rule. What prefixes are contracted by a short dash over the following sign? What by a short dash below? What by a vertical line written downwards through the following sign? What by a horizontal line? Write *sub, sup*. Write *extra, extre, extri*. Write *intro, enter*. Write *contra, contri, contro, counter*. Write the table of double prefixes. How may they be employed in words? Write list of irregular prefixes. Give examples of how *above* and *over* are written. *Under* and *below?* Give examples.

LESSON VI.
ON CONTRACTED AFFIXES.

In addition to the list of prefixes given in the preceding lesson, there are a number of affixes, the contraction of which will be found to materially shorten the writing. After the rules, or basis of the contracted form of writing, have been acquired, the employment of these contracted affixes will only be occasionally necessary; as in the majority of cases, by applying the rules, the word will be abbreviated before the affix has been reached. It is well, however, for the student to become thoroughly familiar with their forms; so, that when occasion demands their use, there need be no hesitancy in employing them. They will be found to be especially advantageous in writing words of two syllables.

NESS, which terminates many words, may be represented by the *n* sign ; thus: *goodness* *coldness*

FULL may be represented by the *f* sign ; thus: *graceful* ; *tearful.*

LESS may be represented by the *l* sign ; thus: *homeless* ; *priceless*

CIAN, TION, CION, SION may be contracted by dropping the nasal combinations and using the *sh* sign joined to the remainder of the word; thus: *silician* *action* *mission*

ABLE, IBLE may be represented by the *b* sign ; thus: *durable* *intelligible*

TATIVE may be represented by the signs *tv* ; thus: *meditative*

LATIVE may be represented by the signs *lv* ; thus: *relative*

BILITY may be represented by the signs *bt* ; thus: *debility* *ability*

The following double affixes may be contracted by joining the contracted signs of the simple affixes; thus FULLY may be represented by as *tastefully* ; FULLNESS by the signs *fn* as *hatefulness*. LESSLY and OUSLY may be represented by the signs *ly* as *heedlessly* ; *previously* . LESSNESS by *ln* as *senselessness* . IVENESS by *vn* as *repulsiveness* . OUSNESS is indicated by *sn* as *seriousness* . ABLENESS is indicated by *bn* as in *sociableness* . SCIOUSNESS, TIOUSNESS, SEOUSNESS by *shn* ; and GEOUSNESS, DEOUSNESS by *jn* as *consciousness* ; *hideousness*.

TABLE OF CONTRACTED AFFIXES.

AFFIXES.	SIGN.	EXAMPLE.	APL'N.
Ness,	)	business,	
Full,	\	useful,	
Ment,	(	torment,	
Less,	/	useless,	
Clan, tion, cion, sion,	⌒	Grecian, omission,	
Able, ible,	|	notable, terrible,	

DOUBLE AFFIXES.

Ably, ibly,	↓	notably, terribly,	
Lative,	∧	relative,	
Tative,		representative,	
Bility,	L	debility,	
Fully,	∪	usefully,	
Fullness,	)	usefulness,	
Lessly, lously,	/	endlessly, seduously,	
Lessness,	∽	uselessly,	
Iveness,		attractiveness,	
Ousness,		nervousness,	
Ableness,		desirableness,	
Sciousness, }		consciousness, }	
Tiousness, }		fictitiousness, }	
Deousness, }		hideousness, }	
Geousness, }		gorgeousness, }	

READING EXERCISE XI.
On Contracted Affixes.

WRITING EXERCISE XI.
ON CONTRACTED PREFIXES.

Business, uneasiness, kindness, blindness, goodness, greatness, wickedness, coldness, softness, hardness. Ornament, refinement, refreshment, retirement, measurement, discernment, enchantment, statement, temperament. Faultless, useless, regardless, shapeless, homeless, shameless, sinless, merciless, artless, faithless, speechless. Graceful, hurtful, skillful, disgraceful, doleful, sorrowful, joyful, lawful, faithful, respectful, hopeful, trustful. Movable, navigable, notable, palatable, passable, peaceable, preferable, sociable, tenable. Position, occasion, contraction, sanction, Grecian, passion, question, suspicion, motion, pension. Truthfully, mercifully, sorrowfully, tastefully, skillfully, revengefully, awfully, gracefully, spitefully, successfully. Cheerfulness, hopefulness, pitifulness, painfulness, peacefulness, spitefulness, thankfulness, truthfulness, hatefulness, skillfulness. Hopelessly, senselessly, painlessly, listlessly, pitilessly. Ruthlessness, senselessness, shamelessness, thanklessness, lawlessness, heartlessness. Defectiveness, submissiveness, effectiveness, persuasiveness, relativeness, repulsiveness, destructiveness, delusiveness. Feasibleness, disagreeableness, sociableness, unreasonableness, desirableness. Argumentative, meditative, representative, recitative, demonstrative. Mutability, sociability, fallibility, tractability, malleability. Graciousness, maliciousness, ferociousness, facetiousness, fictitiousness. Frivolousness, mysteriousness, imperiousness, seriousness, deliriousness.

READING EXERCISE XII.

WRITING EXERCISE XII.

1 The hope*less* and meditative represen*tative* of a noble house reflected on the muta*bility* of all things human.

2 In the delirio*usness* of excite*ment*, the grace*less* youth, heedless of observa*tion*, reckl*essly* quaffed the palat*able* refresh*ments*.

3 The desira*bleness* of the loca*tion* made amends for the defect*iveness* of the tene*ment*.

4 The natural cheer*fulness* and socia*bility* of the young man's tempera*ment*, combined with his truth*fulness*, were the reasons of his rapid advance*ment* to an enviable posi*tion*.

5 It is use*less* to enter into any busi*ness* engage*ment* for which one has no a*bility*, or which is disagreeable.

6 The serio*usness* of the occa*sion* demanded that all sense*less* frivolous*ness* and extravagant show should be di*s*pensed with.

7 The beauti*ful* orna*ment* was hope*lessly* crushed into a shape*less* mass by the care*lessness* of the awkward waiter.

8 The law*less* robber leaned list*lessly* against the wall and displayed the utmost heart*lessness* while looking upon the scene of the terri*ble* disaster.

9 The art*less* heir was fault*lessly* attired, and with the ut*most* socia*bility* moved grace*fully* among his guests and contributed much to the enjoy*ment* of the entertain*ment*.

10 The medi*tative* client was possessed at times of an argumen*tative* turn of mind, and on that occa*sion* did not display his usual mysterio*usness* of deport*ment*.

REVIEW OF LESSON FIFTH.

Give sign of *ment, ness, full, less,* &c. How are double affixes written? Give list of single affixes? Give list of double affixes? How may the latter be employed? Give example with *fully, fullness,* &c. In what words will the use of the contracted affixes be found most advantageous. How are *cian, tion, cion, sion,* written at end of word? *Able,* and *ible? Lessly, lously? Ousness, lessness?*

LESSON VI.

SCALE ILLUSTRATING THE MANNER OF CONTRACTION ON THE VOWEL AND COMBINATION SIGNS.

$$\frac{i, \breve{e}, Y,}{\bar{a}, e} \quad \frac{\bar{o}, au}{oo, uh} \quad \text{—ah, ow.} \quad \text{—+an, en.} \quad \text{—+on, un.}$$

The above scale represents the manner in which words may be abbreviated on the vowel sounds and combinations. On this simple formula, rests the basis of all the rules for contractions. Instead of memorizing thousands of arbitrary word-signs, as in other methods, this system is abbreviated principally by the above scale. The short line represents a part of the word written until a certain vowel sound or combination has been reached, when the remainder of the word is left unwritten, and the next word placed in position to the written part to indicate the sound on which the word is abbreviated, and thus, with the assistance of the general context, supplying the remainder of the word. When the abbreviation rests upon the long ā sound, the next word is written as far below the incomplete word as the space indicated in the scale, and directly under the last sign of the written part of the word. Long ē is written a similar distance below, but a little to the right of the incomplete word. To illustrate the above: *A complaint was made against the boy,* would be abbreviated in this way: *A compl   m   the boy;* or in short-hand,   *was   against*

The words *was* and *against* being placed at a certain distance below indicates that the next sign following the L and M signs is ā. In like manner in the sentence: *Harry peeled the apple,* the ē sign in *peeled* is abbreviated by placing the word following beneath, a little to the right; thus: *Harry p   apple the*

Words containing i, ĕ or Y sounds, may be contracted on them by writing the next word as far above the last sign of the written part of the word to be contracted, as is indicated in the scale; i immediately above and the ĕ or Y a little to the right; thus: *Time flies quickly,   Are you going to the city?*

When it is desired to contract words on the *oo* and *uh* signs, write the next word close below the last sign of the incomplete word as indicated in the scale, and directly under the last written sign for *oo*   : a little to the right for the *uh* sign   ; thus: *Look not upon the wine,*

The little bird has lost its nest,

Words are contracted on the ō and *au* signs in a manner just the reverse of the rule given for ōō and *uh*; the next word being placed directly *above* the last sign of the written word for ō, and a little to the right for *au;* thus: *Blessed are they that mourn, for they shall be comforted,*   *You were the cause of this,*

To abbreviate on the *ah* and *ow* sounds, write the next word on the same line as the incomplete word, and in close proximity to it for the *ah* sign, and a trifle to the right for the *ow;* thus: *John is a bad boy,*   . *The clouds in the sky,*

Words containing the combinations *an, en* are contracted on them by writing the word following, through the last written sign of the incomplete word, at the same distance from the end of it as is indicated in the scale; thus: *The intelligence of the people is the security of the nation.* — Again I say to you, *countrymen.*

The contractions on the *on, un* sounds differ from the foregoing only in writing the following word closer to the end of the sign as represented in the scale; thus: *Kind hearts are more than coronets, and simple faith than Norman blood.*

As *am, em, om, um,* when written before *p* and *b* are nasal combinations, they are contracted in the same manner as *an, en, on, un.* When a word of two or more syllables terminates with any of the combinations, it is not necessary to either write or contract it as the remainder of the word will indicate it; thus: *situation*, *protection*, *execution*

The last word in a sentence may be contracted by placing a dot below, above or in proximity to the written part of the word according to the vowel sign to be contracted; thus: *You have come at last,* , and a little dash through the end of the word to indicate the combinations; thus: *It is proof sufficient,* . In cases where the final sign of the incomplete word and the initial sign of the following one run in the same direction, the contraction may also be indicated by a dot placed at the proper distance above, below, or in proximity to the written part; or a little dash written through the end, in cases where the contraction depends on the combination; thus: *United we stand, divided we fall,*

In contracting the word *stand* on the combination *an*, the last written sign is *t*, and the initial sign of *divided*, the position word, being *d*, it is impossible to intersect them, as both run in the same direction. We therefore cross the end of the *t* sign with a little dash, to indicate the contraction, and write the next word on the same line.

Owing to the awkward appearance of the writing, it is not generally advisable to abbreviate two consecutive words by position, especially if written one above the other. In such cases, the contraction of the second one may be indicated by a dot instead of by the following word. Final vowel signs should seldom be cut off, as they can generally be written as quickly as the pen could be raised to contract them by position.

Words separated by a comma may be placed in position to each other, but not when separated by any other punctuation mark. In contracting by position, it must be remembered that the distance is calculated from above or below the *end* of the final sign of the incomplete word; thus: *He picked up a piece of money,* ⌣ 17 . ⌒ ⌣ ⌒ , the next word *up* being placed a certain distance above the *end* of the *p* sign, in *picked*, and not a certain distance from its commencement.

READING EXERCISE XIII.
CONTRACTIONS ON ă AND ĕ.

ă, ĕ

WRITING EXERCISE XIII.
CONTRACTIONS ON ă AND ĕ.

ă, ĕ

Art is the application of knowledge to a practical end. Prayer should be the key of the day and the lock of the night. Education is the cheap defense of nations. Maintain the place where thou standest. There is but one easy place in the world, and that is the grave. Blessed are the meek, for they shall possess the land. Blessed are the clean of heart, for they shall see God. A penny saved is a penny gained. No one is placed on earth to do nothing; there is a state, an office, a labor for each. He is truly great who has great charity. No accusations should be advanced except upon proof sufficient to maintain them. 'Tis as much of a trade to make a book as to make a watch; there's something more than wit necessary to make an author. In this world of change, naught which comes stays, and naught which goes is lost. Situations are like skeins of thread or silk; to make the most of them we need only to take them by the right end. Faith is not a belief that we are saved, but that we are loved. Every one makes his own reputation; the world only puts on the stamp. Language is the close-fitting dress of thought. Proverbs are the cream of a nation's thought. Great names degrade instead of elevate those who do not know how to sustain them. 'Tis late before the brave despair. A straw or a feather sustains itself long in the air. The truly brave are soft of heart and eyes.

READING EXERCISE XIV.
Contractions on i, ĕ or I.
i, ĕ, I

WRITING EXERCISE XIV.
CONTRACTIONS ON i, ĕ OR Ĭ.
i, ĕ, Ĭ

Trifles make perfection, but *perfection* is no trifle. It is said of office-holders that they rarely die and never resign. Tears are the showers that fertilize the world. Thinking is the talking of the soul with itself. I would rather be right than President. How far that little candle throws its beam! so shines a good deed in a naughty world. The happiest women, like the happiest nations, have no history. Sweet mercy is nobility's true badge. United we stand, divided we fall. Writing with a pencil is like speaking with a low voice. Youth should be a savings bank. We are always looking into the future, but we see only the past. We should count time by heart-throbs. Houses are built to live in, not to look on; therefore, let use be preferred before uniformity except where both can be had. It is not true that heavy sorrows diminish our sensibilities to trifling pains. In religion, as in every other profession, practicing is the great thing. If you cannot bring your condition to your mind, bring your mind to your *condition*. When a man asks your advice, he generally wants your praise. Not only strike while the iron is hot, but make it hot by striking. The intelligence of the people is the security of the nation. He is nearest to the gods who knows how to be silent, even though he is in the right. Whatever you do, do it willingly. A boy that is whipped at school never learns his lesson well. Our characters are the inscriptions we are making on the hearts of those who know, and who will survive us.

READING EXERCISE XV.
Contractions on *oo*, *uh*.

oo, uh

WRITING EXERCISE XV.

CONTRACTIONS ON *oo, uh.*

---
oo, uh

We can refute assertions, but who can refute silence? A certain statesman has said: Youth is a blunder, manhood a struggle, old age a regret. Truth fears nothing but concealment. A word fitly spoken is like apples of gold in pictures of silver. Ridicule is the test of truth. Always look on the bright side. Reading makes a full man. We loose the peace of years when we hunt after the rapture of moments. Blessed are the poor in spirit, for theirs is the Kingdom of Heaven. People seldom improve when they have no other model but themselves to copy after. Instruction ends in the school-room, but education ends only with life. Religion is the best armor a man can have, but the worst cloak. A failure in a good cause is better than a triumph in a bad one. Distrust him who talks much of his honesty. In youth we feel the richer for every new illusion; in mature years for every one we lose. Flowers are banners of the vegetable world which march in various and splendid triumph before the coming of the fruits. The gratitude of the lowly is precious. Genius makes its observations in short-hand; talent writes them out in long-hand. God has put something noble and good into every heart which His hand has created.

READING EXERCISE XVI.

Contractions on ŏ and *au*.

___ŏ, *au*___

(shorthand content)

WRITING EXERCISE XVI.

CONTRACTIONS ON ŏ AND *au*.

ŏ. *au*

The gratitude of the lowly is precious. The hand that rocks the cradle rules the world. A broken-down scholar is like a razor without a handle. Thought is the property of those only who can entertain it. An apt quotation is as good as an original remark. Laws are like cobwebs, where the small flies are caught, and the great break through. We must do everything for others; if only to divert our minds from what they fail to do for us. Sorrows are our best educators. How far that little candle throws its beam. The flower of meekness grows on a stem of grace. There is in all this cold and hollow world, no fount of strong, deathless love save that within a mother's heart. A delicate thought is a flower of the mind. Look at those you are talking to, never at those you are talking of. Words at the touch of the poet blossom into poetry. Man is the glory, jest and riddle of the world. On every height there lies repose. The generous heart should scorn a pleasure which gives others pain. Woman, like gold, is a legal tender the world over. Philosophy is the science of realities. Doubt is the accusing attorney in the Court of Truth. The flowers of rhetoric are only acceptable when backed by the evergreens of truth and sense. The granite statue, rough hewn though it be, is far more imposing in its simple and stern, though rude proportions, than the plaster-cast, however elaborately wrought and gilded.

READING EXERCISE XVII.
Contractions on *ah, ow.*

——*ah, ow*

[Shorthand content]

WRITING EXERCISE XVII.

Contractions on *ah, ow.*

———*ah, ow*

The greatest homage we can pay to truth is to use it. Shorthand should be put into practical use. To have ideas is to gather flowers; to think is to weave them into garlands. Society is like a large piece of frozen water; and skating well is the great art of social life. The ideal of friendship is to feel as one while remaining two. Contact with a high-minded woman is good for the life of any man. To make home pleasant and attractive should be the aim of every man. Let the dead past bury its dead. Try to discharge your duty under all circumstances. A man is educated who knows how to apply his education to all practical purposes. We are all busy—busy writing epitaphs. We do not let a day pass without doing something in this line; and we are all busy, not in writing epitaphs for others, but in writing our own. There is a past which is gone forever, but there is a future which is all our own. I count this thing to be grandly true. We mount to the summit round by round. Never be cast down by trifles. "What ranger of the clouds can dare, proud mountain king! with thee compare." Shout aloud the praises of our king.

READING EXERCISE XVIII.

Contractions on *an, en, in.*

—✝—*an, en, in*

[shorthand content]

WRITING EXERCISE XVIII.

Contractions on *an, en, in.*

———┼-*an, en, in.*

Experience is a fine word for suffering. Aim at excellence and excellence will be attained. This is the great secret of success and emulation. "I cannot do it" never accomplished anything. "I will try," has wrought wonders. Each substance of a grief hath twenty shadows which show like grief itself, but are not so. Sow good services, sweet remembrances will grow from them. It is better to praise a man for his virtues although they may be few and his faults many, than to condemn him for his faults and forget his virtues. Strength of mind is exercise, not rest. Reading makes a full man, conference a ready man, and writing an exact man.- I can understand the things that afflict mankind, but I often marvel at those which console. The intelligence of the people is the security of the nation. Whoever thinks of life as something that could be without religion is yet in deadly ignorance of both. The sun which ripens the corn and fills the succulent herb with nutriment also pencils with beauty the violet and the rose. The honorable gentleman is indebted to his memory for his wit, and to his imagination for his facts. To understand the present, we must study the productive influences of the past.

READING EXERCISE XIX.

CONTRACTIONS ON *on, un.*

——┼*on, un.*

[shorthand exercise]

WRITING EXERCISE XIX.

CONTRACTIONS ON *on, un.*

———┼*on, un.*

Passio*ns* are like*n*ed best to floods and streams; the shallow murmur, but the deep are dumb. It will afford sweeter happi*n*ess in the hour of death to have wiped away one tear from one check of sorrow, than to have ruled a*n* empire, or to have co*n*quered millio*ns*, or enslaved the world. Accompa*ny* your own flag throughout the world under the prote*ction* of your own ca*n*non. Kind hearts are more than coro*n*ets, and si*m*ple faith than Norma*n* blood. There is a ca*non* of comm*on* sense which should rule in everything. Genius is of the soul, talent of the understanding; genius is warm, tale*n*t is passio*n*less. Without genius there is no intui*tion*, no inspira*tion;* without talent no execu*tion*; genius inv*en*ts, talent accomplishes. Genius gives the substa*n*ce; talent works it up under the eye, or rather the feeling of genius. Genius is emotio*n*al, tale*n*t intellectual; hence, genius is creative, and talent instrume*n*tal. Put not your trust in mo*n*ey, but put your mo*n*ey in trust. It is impossible to love a second time those we have really ceased to love. There may be tale*n*t without position, but there is no posi*tion* without some kind of talent.

REVIEW OF LESSON SIXTH.

On what sounds may the corresponding style of short hand be contracted? How may words be contracted on the a and e sounds? How on the i, ŏ and ĭ? How on the oo, uh sounds? How on the o, au sounds? How on ah, ow? How may words be contracted on the *an, en* combinations? How on the *on, un* combinations? How may the last word in a sentence be contracted? Is it advisable to contract a word on the last sign? Why not? In abbreviating by position, is the distance estimated from the *beginning* or *end* of the sign? In case where the last sign of the incomplete word and the initial sign of the following word run in parallel directions, what is done? Give examples. When *an, en, m, un* come before *p* and *b*, how are they contracted? When a word of two or more syllables terminates with any of the combinations, what is done with the latter? May words separated by a comma be placed in position to each other when abbreviating? By any other punctuation mark?

READING EXERCISE XX.
The Snow of Age.

WRITING EXERCISE XX.

THE SNOW OF AGE.

"No snow falls lighter than the snow of age, but none is heavier, for it never melts."

The figure is by no means novel, but the closing part of the sentence is new, as well as emphatic. The Scriptures represent age by the almond tree, which bears blossoms of the purest white. "The almond tree shall flourish"—the head shall be hoary. Dickens says of one of his characters, whose hair was turning gray, that it looked as if Time had lightly splashed his snows upon it in passing.

"It never melts"—no, never. Age is inexorable. Its wheels must move onward—they know no retrograde movement. The old man may sit and sing, "I would I were a boy again," but he grows older as he sings. He may read of the elixir of youth, but he cannot find it; he may sigh for the secrets of that alchemy which is able to make him young again, but sighing brings it not. He may gaze backward with an eye of longing upon the rosy scenes of early years, as one who gazes on his home from the deck

THE SNOW OF AGE.

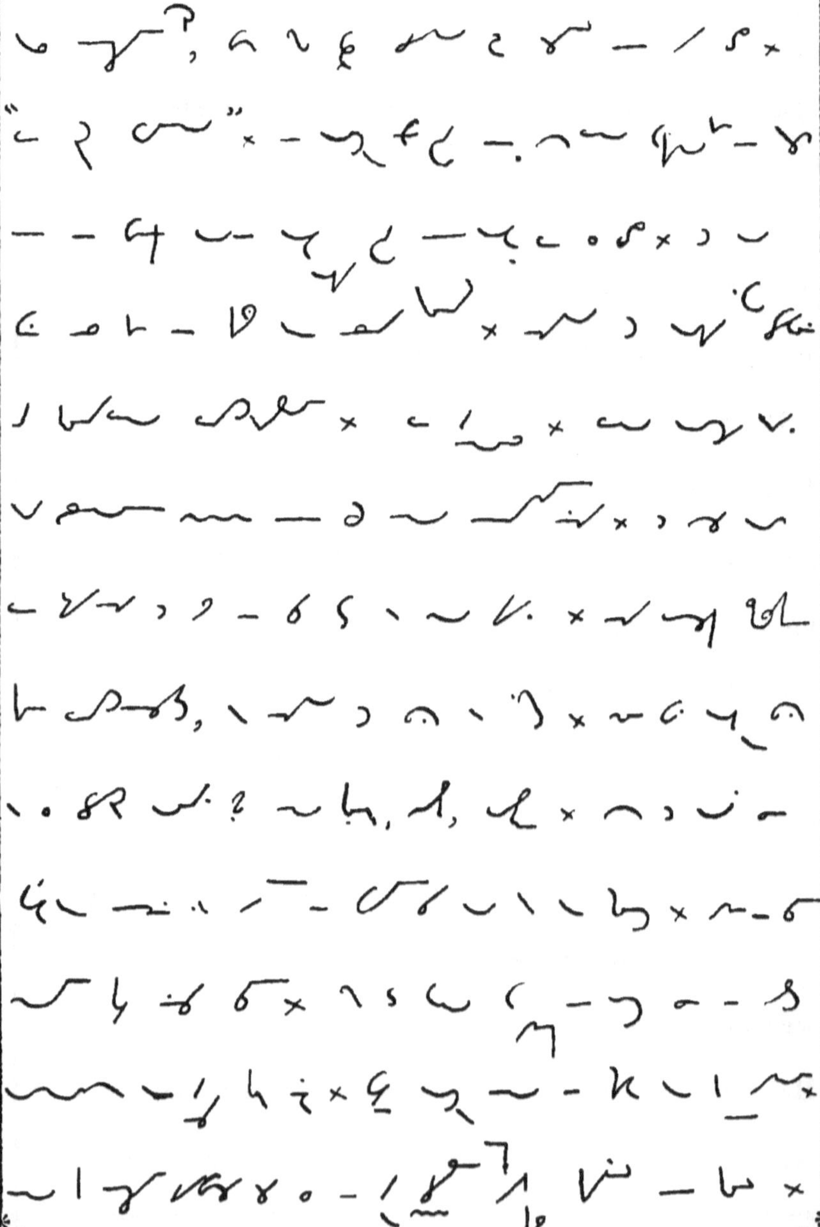

THE SNOW OF AGE.

of a departing ship, which every moment carries him farther and farther away.

"It never melts." The snow of winter comes and sheds its white blessings upon the valley and the mountains, but soon the sweet spring comes and smiles it all away. Not so with that upon the brow of the tottering veteran. There is no spring whose warmth can penetrate its eternal frost. It came to stay. Its single flakes fell unnoticed—and now it is drifted there. We shall see it increase until we lay the old man in his grave. There it shall be absorbed by the eternal darkness, for there is no age in heaven.

Yet why speak of age in a mournful strain? It is beautiful, honorable, eloquent. Should we sigh at the proximity of death, when life and the world are so full of emptiness? Let the old exult because they are old. If any must weep, let it be the young at the long succession of cares that are before them. Welcome the snow, for it is the emblem of peace and of rest. It is but a temporal crown which shall fall at the gates of Paradise, to be replaced by a brighter and a better.

READING EXERCISE XXI.

Golden Grains.

WRITING EXERCISE XXI.

GOLDEN GRAINS.

Selected from various orations by James A. Garfield.

1. Be fit for more than the thing you are now doing.
2. Things do not turn up in this world until somebody turns them up.
3. If the power to do hard work is not talent, it is the best possible substitute for it.
4. It is no honor or profit merely to appear in the arena. The wreath is for those who contend.
5. Many books we can read in a railroad car and feel a harmony between the rushing of the train and the haste of the author.
6. Our national safety demands that the fountains of political power shall be made pure by intelligence and kept pure by vigilance.
7. In order to have any success in life—any worthy success—you must resolve to carry into your work a fullness of knowledge—not merely a sufficiency, but more than a sufficiency.
8. Young men talk of trusting to the spur of the occasion. That trust is vain. Occasions cannot make spurs. If you expect to wear spurs you must win them. If you wish to use them you must buckle them to your own heels before you go into the fight.
9. Power exhibits itself under two distinct forms—strength and force—each possessing peculiar qualities and perfect in its own sphere. Strength is typified by the oak, the rock, the mountain. Force embodies itself in the cataract, the tempest, the thunderbolt.
10. From the genius of our Government, the pathway to honorable distinction lies open to all. No post of honor so high but the poorest boy may hope to reach it. It is the pride of every American that many cherished names, at whose mention our hearts beat with a quicker bound, were worn by the sons of poverty, who conquered obscurity and became fixed stars in our firmament.

READING EXERCISE XXII.

Abraham Lincoln.

WRITING EXERCISE XXII.

ABRAHAM LINCOLN.

The analysis of Mr. Lincoln's character is difficult, on account of its symmetry. Its comprehension is to us impossible, on account of its immensity, for a man can be comprehended only by his peers. Though we may not get its altitude, nor measure its girth, nor fathom its depths, nor estimate its richness, we may get somewhat of the impress of its purity, the inspiration of its heroism, and the impulse of its power. It was centered about a few strong points. His moral sense, his reason, and his common sense, were the three fixed points through which the perfect circle of his character was drawn—the sacred trinity of his great manhood. Had he lacked either of these he would have failed, and we would have been buried in the ruins of a Republic. Without the first, he would have been a villian; without the second, a bigot or a fool; without the third, a fanatic or a dreamer. With them all, he was Abraham Lincoln.

He was the representative character of this age. He incarnated the *ideal* Republic. No other man ever so fully embodied the purposes, the affections and the power of the people. He came up among us; he was one of us. His birth, his education, his habits, his motives, his feelings, and his ambitions were all our own. Had he been born among hereditary aristocrats, he would not have been *our* President; but born in the cabin and reared in the field and in the forest, he became the Great Commoner. The classics of the schools might have polished him, but

ABRAHAM LINCOLN.

[Page of shorthand notation]

ABRAHAM LINCOLN.

they would have separated him from us. But trained in the common school of adversity, his calloused palms never slipped from the poor man's hand. A child of the people, he was accessible in the White House as he had been in the cabin.

There are many noble heroes who illumine the darkness behind us with the radiance of some single virtue, but among them all I see no Lincoln. He is radiant with all the great virtues, and his memory shall shed a glory upon this age that *shall fill the eye of men* as they look into history. An administrator, he saved the nation in the perils of unparalleled *civil* war. A statesman, he justified his measures by their success. A philanthropist, he gave liberty to one race and salvation to another. A moralist, he bowed from the summit of human power to the foot of the cross, and became a Christain. A moralist, he exercised mercy under the most absolute abeyance to law. A leader, he was no partisan. A commander, he was untainted with blood. A ruler in desperate times, he was unsullied with crime. A man, he has left no word of passion, no thought of malice, no trick of craft, no act of jealousy, no purpose of selfish ambition. Thus perfected, without a model and without a peer, he was dropped into these troubled years to adorn and embellish all that is good and all that is great in our humanity, and to present to all coming time the representative of the divine idea of Free Government.

READING EXERCISE XXIII.

Eulogy on Lafayette.

READING EXERCISE XXIII.

Eulogy on Lafayette.

While we bring our offerings for the mighty of our own land, shall we not remember the chivalrous spirits of other shores, who shared with them the hour of weakness and woe? Pile to the clouds the majestic columns of glory; let the lips of those who can speak well, hallow each spot where the bones of our bold repose, but forget not those who, with our bold, went out to battle. Among these men of noble daring there was one, a young and gallant stranger, who left the blushing vinehills of his delightful France. The people whom he came to succor were not his people; he knew them only in the melancholy story of their wrongs. He was no mercenary wretch, striving for the spoils of the vanquished; the palace acknowledged him for its lord, and the valleys yielded him their increase. He was no nameless man, staking life for reputation; he ranked among nobles and looked unawed upon kings. He was no friendless outcast, seeking for a grave to hide his cold heart; he was girdled by the companions of his childhood; his kinsmen were about him; his wife was before him.

Yet from all these he turned away and came. Like a lofty tree, that shakes down its green glories to battle with the winter's storm, he flung aside the trappings of place and pride to crusade

EULOGY ON LAFAYETTE.

EULOGY ON LAFAYETTE.

for Freedom, in Freedom's holy land. He came; but not in the day of successful rebellion; not when the new-risen sun of Independence had burst the cloud of time, and careered to its place in the heavens. He came when darkness curtained the hills, and the tempest was abroad in its anger; when the plough stood still in the field of promise, and briers cumbered the garden of beauty; when fathers were dying, and mothers were weeping over them; when the wife was binding up the gashed bosom of the husband, and the maiden was wiping the death damp from the brow of her lover. He came when the brave began to fear the power of man, and the pious to doubt the favor of God. It was then that this man joined the ranks of a revolted people. Freedom's little phalanx bade him a grateful welcome. With them he courted the battle's rage; with theirs, his arm was lifted; with theirs, his blood was shed. Long and doubtful was the conflict. At length kind Heaven smiled on the good cause, and the beaten invaders fled. The profane were driven from the temple of liberty, and at her pure shrine, the pilgrim warrior, with his adored commander, knelt and worshipped. Leaving there his offering, the incense of an uncorrupted spirit, he at length arose, and, crowned with benedictions, turned his happy feet toward his long-deserted home.

After nearly fifty years he has come again. Can mortal tongue

EULOGY ON LAFAYETTE

EULOGY ON LAFAYETTE.

tell, can mortal heart feel the sublimity of that coming? Exulting millions rejoice in it; and the long, loud, transporting shout, like the mingling of many winds, rolls on, undying, to Freedom's furthest mountains. A congregated nation comes around him. Old men bless him, and children reverence him. The lovely come out to look upon him; the learned deck their halls to greet him; the rulers of the land rise up to do him homage. How his full heart labors! He views the rusting trophies of departed days; he treads upon the high places where his brethren moulder; he bends before the tomb of his father; his words are tears, the speech of sad remembrance. But he looks around upon a ransomed land and a joyous race; he beholds the blessings, those trophies secured, for which those brethren died, for which that father lived; and again his words are tears, the eloquence of gratitude and joy.

Of all the myriads that have come and gone, what cherished memories ever ruled an hour like this. Many have struck the redeeming blow for their own freedom; but who, like this man, has bared his own bosom in the cause of strangers? Others have lived in the love of their own people; but who, like this man, has drunk his sweetest cup of welcome with another? Matchless chief! Oblivion shall never shroud his splendor; and coming generations shall repeat the beloved name of Lafayette.

REMARKS ON THE USE OF WORD-SIGNS.

The following pages will be found to contain a list of the most frequently recurring phrases, and their combination into phraseograms. There is, also, given a page of word-signs formed from words which cannot be contracted very briefly by rule, together with a list of common abbreviations and their corresponding abbreviations in short-hand. The advantage gained by forming the word-phrases into combinations is, that they can be written together without raising the pen; whereas, if abbreviated by rule, each word of the phrase would have to be written separately. As there are not more than a few hundred of them in all, the memory will not be taxed to any great extent in acquiring them. No effort should be made to memorize them, but the learner should, instead, write each page many times until they become familiar enough to him to adopt into his writing. Should he desire to carry this mode of abbreviations still further, he can do so by writing only the principal sounds of the words contained in other phrases. In addition to these printed lists, there are special contractions used in every profession and every department of business. For instance, the clergyman, the lawyer, the merchant, the book-keeper, the telegraph operator, &c., will each use special abbreviations in his long-hand writing which he may carry with advantage into his short-hand work, by writing these contractions in corresponding phonographic characters.

As figures may be written very rapidly, no special signs are given for them. *First, second, third, fourth, fifth, &c.* may be written 1, 2, 3, 4, 5, &c., and *once, twice, thrice, &c.* 1̄, 2̄, 3̄, &c.

LIST OF FAMILIAR PHRASES.

- a few days ago.
- a few moments ago.
- a short time ago.
- a long time ago.
- a short space of time.
- at all events.
- at present.
- all at once.
- at all times.
- at the time.
- at the same time.
- at that time.
- at least.
- as well as.
- as soon as.
- as good as.
- as great as.
- as much as.
- as far as.
- as far as it goes.
- as follows.
- after you went away.
- after all that.
- after that time.
- and so forth.
- again and again.
- able to be.
- able to be out.
- able to have.
- able to do.
- able to see.
- because of it.
- because it is not.
- because it is so.
- by all means.
- by the.
- by means of.
- by every means.
- by no means.
- by some means.

	bye and bye.		dear brethren.
	by right.		dear friend.
	can be.		every now and then.
	can it be.		every one.
	can it be possible.		everything.
	can have been.		everything else.
	cannot.		every time.
	cannot be.		everywhere.
	cannot have been.		far from it.
	could not be.		far be it from me.
	could not have been.		for all that.
	do not.		forever and ever.
	do you.		for instance.
	do you not.		for example,
	did you.		from time to time.
	did you not.		gentlemen of the jury.
	dear sir.		he can.
	dear madam.		he can be.
	dearly beloved.		he cannot be.
	dearly beloved brethren		he had been.

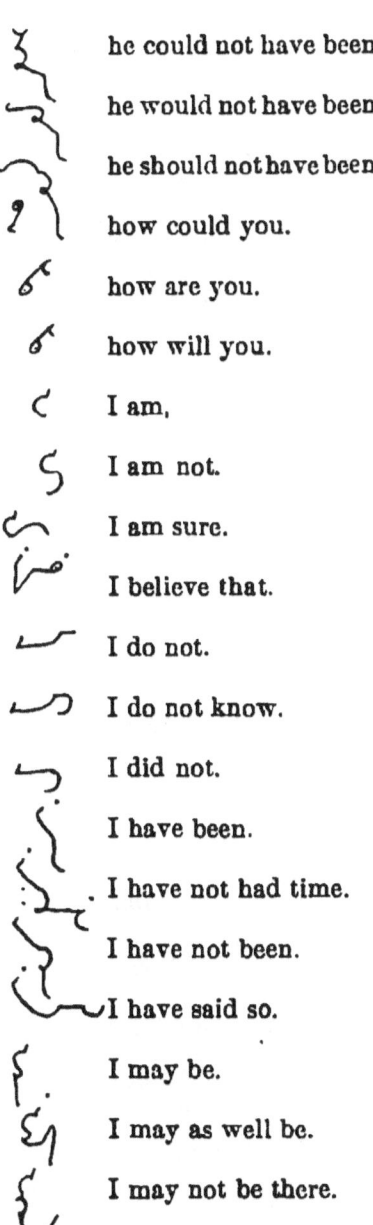

he could not have been
he would not have been
he should not have been
how could you.
how are you.
how will you.
I am,
I am not.
I am sure.
I believe that.
I do not.
I do not know.
I did not.
I have been.
I have not had time.
I have not been.
I have said so.
I may be.
I may as well be.
I may not be there.

I know it to be so.
I might have been.
I must be.
I shall not be able to go
I might have said so.
I never said so.
I must say.
I was not.
I will.
I will not.
I would.
I would not be.
if it is to be.
if it is possible.
if he did.
if they were.
if we were.
if you were.
if you do.
in the meantime.

	in fact.		it will not be.
	in order to get it.		it will never be.
	in the course of.		it would seem.
	inasmuch as.		just as long as.
	in spite of.		just as well as.
	in general.		know it.
	in such a manner.		know all about it.
	in some degree.		know there is.
	it is.		many as possible.
	it is not.		many more.
	it appears to be.		more and more.
	it could not be.		most likely to be.
	it has been.		no better.
	it would have been.		no doubt.
	it ought to have been.		no such thing.
	it is said to be.		not knowing.
	it is so.		neither of them.
	it is true.		not in the least.
	it will.		not only.
	it will be.		of all.

	of it.		point of view.
	of him.		present day.
	of her.		quite likely.
	of them.		quite enough of it.
	of that.		railroad.
	of this.		say so.
	of which.		say to them.
	of course.		say unto you.
	of course it must be.		seems to be.
	on hand.		see how.
	on account.		see how he can.
	on account of.		shall be.
	on this account.		shall not be.
	on the contrary.		shall not have been.
	on this occasion.		should have been.
	one another.		so that.
	ought not to have been		so as to be.
	out of the way.		so far as you can.
	police court.		so there should be.
	prisoner at the bar.		so very little.

	some of them.		to do as.
	something has been said		to do so.
	such as can.		to have been.
	that is not.		to be sure.
	that is the question.		to do something.
	that is to say.		to take care.
	there can be no doubt.		to me.
	there are.		to him.
	therefore.		to them.
	there has been.		to it.
	there is no objection.		to put.
	there ought to be.		to give.
	they may not go.		we know.
	they may as well.		we do not know.
	this is well known.		we have been.
	this may be.		we shall be.
	to be.		we are not.
	to be able to.		we were.
	to do this.		we were there.
	to do it.		we can go.

	we have had.		who would not be.
	we will.		what is it.
	we will be.		with which.
	we will be sure.		with respect.
	we will try.		you are.
	were they.		you are not.
	were we.		you do not.
	were you.		you will.
	which are.		you will not be.
	which are now.		you must be.
	which has been.		you have not been.
	which is not.		you should be.
	which will be.		you shall be.
	who are.		you could be.
	who are not.		yours truly.
	who can be.		yours respectfully.
	who is it.		yours at hand.

LIST OF WORDS NOT CONTRACTED BY RULE.

ʒ	acknowledge.		impossible.
	acquainted.		immediate.
	advertise.		indignity.
	afternoon.		irregular.
	afterwards.		language.
	already.		magnificent.
	candidate.		magnitude.
	character.		meanwhile.
	characterize.		nevertheless.
	children.		notwithstanding.
	churchyard.		nowadays.
	circumstance.		opposite.
	congressman.		possible.
	difficult.		peculiar.
	difference.		recognition.
	especially.		recovered
	everywhere.		require.
	excommunicate.		several.
	establish.		scripture.
	establishment.		universe.
	forward.		universal.
	government.		upward.

CONTRACTIONS ON COMMON ABBREVIATIONS.

A		Answer.	App.		Appendix.
A. M.		Beforenoon; Master of Arts.	Archd.		Archdeacon.
A. B.		Bachelor of Arts	Archb.		Archbishop.
Abv.		Abbreviated.	Arith.		Arithmetic.
Abp.		Archbishop.	Atty.		Attorney.
Act.		Account; Acting.	Av.		Average; Avenue.
A. D.		In the year of our Lord.	B.		But; Bank; Book
Ad.		Adverb.	Bal.		Balance.
Adj.		Adjective; Adjutant.	Bp.		Bishop.
Adm.		Admiral.	Bro.		Brother.
Admr.		Administration.	Breth.		Brethren
Adv.		Advent; Advocate.	Bush.		Bushel.
Agr.		Agriculture.	B. V.		Blessed Virgin.
Agt.		Agent.	B.V.M.		Blessed Virgin Mary.
Amr.		American; America.	C.		Consul; Cent.
Amt.		Amount.	Con.		Conductor.
Anal.		Analysis.	Cap.		Capital.
Anat.		Anatomy.	Cath.		Catholic; Cathedral.
Anon.		Anonymous.	Col.		College; Colony; Column.
Ant.		Antiquities.	Celt.		Celtic

C. C.	⌣. ⌣	County Clerk; Chief Clerk.	D. D.	—. —	Doctor of Divinity.
C. C P.	⌣.⌣	Court of Common Pleas.	Deg.	⌐	Degree.
Ch. C.	⌒	Church of Christ.	Dem.	⌐.	Democrat.
Chron.	✓	Chronicles; Chronology.	Dept.	⌐.	Department.
Cit.	⌣	Citizen	Depon.	⌐ɔ.	Deponent.
Civ.	⌐.	Civil.	Deut.	—.	Deuteronomy.
C. J.	⌣. ⌒	Chief Justice.	D. F.	—. \	Defender of the Faith.
Clk.	⋁.	Clerk.	Diam.	⌐.	Diameter.
Co.	d.	County; Company.	Dict.	⌐z.	Dictionary.
C. O. D.	/.o	Collect on Delivery.	Dim.	⌐.	Diminutive.
Com.	ȼ.	Commissioner; Committee.	Dist.	⌣	District.
Cong.	ƒ	Congress.	Div.	⌐	Division.
Const.	⌣	Constitution.	Doz.	⌣	Dozen.
Cor.	✓	Corinthians.	Dr.	⌐	Doctor; Dear; Debtor.
Cor. C.	✗.⌣	Corresponding Clerk.	E.	⌣.	East.
Cor. Sec.	✗⌐	Corresponding Secretary.	E. E.	⌣. ⌣.	Errors excepted.
Cr.	✓	Creditor.	Eg.	⌐	For example.
C.S.A.	⌣.⌣	Confederate States of Am.	Elec.	⌐	Electric; Electricity.
Cop.	ɋ	Copper; Coptic.	Emp.	⌐.	Emperor; Empress.
Cwt.	⌐	Hundred weight	Ency.	⌐.	Encyclopedia.
Cycl.	⌐	Cyclopedia	Ep.	ʔ	Epistle.

Env.		Envoy; Envelope.
Esq.		Esquire.
Et al.		And others.
Etc.		And so forth.
Fig.		Figure; Figurative.
Fo.		Folio.
Fr.		Franc.
Gen.		General; Genesis.
Gen.		Gentleman.
Geol.		Geology.
Handk.		Handkerchief.
Hhd.		Hogshead.
Hist.		History.
H. M.		Her Majesty.
H. M. S.		Her Majesty's Service.
Hon.		Honorable.
Hort.		Horticulture.
H. R.		House of Representatives.
H. R. H.		His Royal Highness.
i. e.		That is.
Int.		Interest.
Inst.		Present month; Institute.
J.		Judge; Justice.
Jr.		Jury; Junior.
J. A.		Judge Advocate.
J. P.		Justice of the Peace.
L. D.		Doctor of Laws.
K. C. B.		Knight Com'der of the Bath.
K. G.		Knight of the Garter.
K. P.		Knight of St. Patrick.
K. S. G.		Knight of St. George.
L.		Lord; Lady.
Lp.		Ladyship, Lordship.
Lat.		Latitude.
L. C. J.		Lord Chief Justice.
Legis.		Legislature.
Lib.		Librarian.
Lt.		Lieutenant.
Lt. Col.		Lieut. Colonel.
Lt. Gen.		Lieut. General.
Lit.		Literature; Literally.

L L B.	✓✓. ǀ.	Bachelor of Laws.	Mus.	⌣.	Museum.
LL.D.	✓✓—	Doctor of Laws.	Myth.	⌣.	Mythology.
L.S.D.	✓⌣.—	Pounds, shillings and pence.	Naut.	⌢.	Nautical.
M. A.	⌣. ⌢	Master of Arts.	N. B.	⊃. ǀ	Take notice.
Manf.	⌊	Manufacturing.	Nom.	⟩.	Nominative.
Mad.	⌣.	Madam.	Nos.	⟨.	Numbers.
Mlle.	⌢·	Mademoiselle.	N. P.	⊃. ɩ.	Notary Public.
Ms.	⌣.	Manuscript.	N. V. M	⊃. \. ⊂	Nativity of the Virgin Mary.
March.	⌢··	Marchioness.	Obj.	⌒.	Objective.
Marq.	⌢⌢	Marquis.	Obs.	⌒,	Observation; Observatory.
Math.	⌢.	Mathematics.	Obt.	⌒.	Obedient.
Met.	⌣·	Metaphysics.	Olym.	⌢.	Olympic.
Med.	⌣—·	Medicine.	Opt.	⌒.	Optics.
Mem.	⌞.	Memorandum.	Oz.	⌣·	Ounce or Ounces
Mid.	⌣—·	Midshipman.	Pent.	⌞.	Pentecost.
Mil.	⌣.	Military.	Per an.	✓ ⟩.	Per annum.
Min.	⌢.	Minute; Minister	Phar.	✓	Pharmacy.
Mo.	6.	Month. ·	Philos.	⌣·	Philosophy.
Mr.	✓.	Mister	Phren.	✓·	Phrenology.
Mrs	⌢.	Mistress.	Pl.	✓·	Plural.
Mt.	⌣.	Mountain.	Plf.	⋀.	Plaintiff.

P. M.		Postmaster; Afternoon.	Ref.		Reform.
P. O.		Post Office.	Regt.		Regiment.
Pop.		Population.	Rem.		Remarks.
Pp.		Pages.	Rep.		Report; Reporter.
Prop.		Proprietor; Propeller.	Repr.		Represent.
Priv.		Privilege.	Rep.		Republic.
Prof.		Professor.	Rev.		Reverend; Revelation.
Pron.		Pronoun.	Rhet.		Rhetoric.
Prot.		Protestant.	R. S.		Right side.
Pro-tem.		For the time.	Scr.		Scruple.
Prov.		Proverbs, Province.	Sculp		Sculpture.
Pros.		Prosody.	Sec.		Secretary.
P. S.		Postscript.	Sen.		Senior; Senate; Senator.
Pub.		Publisher; Publication.	Serg.		Sergeant.
Ques.		Question.	Servt.		Servant.
Q. B.		Queen's Bench.	S. L.		Solicitor-at-Law
Q. C.		Queen's Council	Sq.		Square.
Qt.		Quart; Quantity.	Vs.		Versus; Against
Qu.		Query.	Vul.		Vulgar; Vulgate
R.		River; Railway.	Wp.		Worship.
Rec.		Received.	Wpf.		Worshipful.
Rect.		Receipt.	Zool.		Zoology.

ABBREVIATION OF PROPER NAMES.

Eng.	England.	Jno.		John.
Eph.	Ephesus.	Jo.		Joseph.
Esth.	Esther.	Kan.		Kansas.
Ezek.	Ezekiel.	Kent.		Kentucky.
Fr.	French; France.	La.		Louisiana.
G. B.	Great Britain.	Lev.		Leviticus.
Geo.	George.	L. I.		Long Island.
Ga.	Georgia.	Lon.		London.
Heb.	Hebrews.	Minn.		Minnesota.
Hin.	Hindostan.	Maj.		Major.
Hung.	Hungary.	Maj Gen.		Major General.
Ia.	Iowa.	Mass.		Massachusetts.
Ice.	Iceland.	Math.		Matthew.
Ill.	Illinois.	M. C.		Member of Congress.
Ire.	Ireland; Irish.	M P.		Member of Parliament.
J.Chr.	Jesus Christ.	M. D.		Doctor of Medicine.
J.H.S.	Jesus Savior of Men.	Me.		Maine.
Jas.	James.	M. E.		Methodist Episcopal.
Jam.	Jamaica.	Mex.		Mexico.
Jer.	Jeremiah.	Miss.		Mississippi.

N. A.	⊃ ⌒	North America.		R. N.	∕ ⊃	Royal Navy.
Nath.	⊃	Nathaniel.		R C.	∕ ⌣	Roman Catholic.
N. B.	⊃ ⎮	New Brunswick.		S. A.	⌣ ⌒	South America.
N. C.	⊃ ⌣	North Carolina.		Sam.	⌐	Samuel.
Neb.	⌐	Nebraska.		Sans.	⌒	Sanscrit.
Nem.	⊃	Nehemiah.		Sax.	⌐	Saxon.
N. F.	⊃ ⟍	Newfoundland.		S. C.	⌣ ⌣	South Carolina.
N. H.	⊃ ·	New Hampshire		Scot.	⌐	Scotland.
N. J.	⊃ ⌒	New Jersey.		Sol.	⌐	Solomon.
N. M.	⊃ ⌐	New Mexico.		Span.	⌐	Spanish.
N. O.	⊃ ○	New Orleans.		Switz.	⌐	Switzerland.
N. Y.	⊃ ⌐	New York.		Tenn.	⌒	Tennessee.
N. Z.	⊃ ⌣	New Zealand.		Tex.	⌐	Texas.
O.	○	Ohio.		Theo.	⌐	Theodore.
Pa.	⌐	Pennsylvania.		Thom.	⌐	Thomas.
P. E. I.	⎮ ⌣ ∕	Prince Edward's Island.		Tim.	⌐	Timothy.
Phila.	⌐	Philadelphia.		Turk.	∕	Turkey; Turkish
Port.	⌐	Portugal.		U. K.	⌣ ∕	United Kingdom
R. I.	∕ ∕	Rhode Island.		U.S.A.	⌣ ⌣ ⌒	United States of America.
R. M.	∕ ⌐	Royal Marines.				

U.S.M. ⌒⌣	(United States Mail.	
U.S.N. ⌒⌣	)United States Navy.	
U. T. ⌒ —	Utah Territory.	
Va. ⟩	Virginia.	
V. C. \⌣	Vice Chancellor.	
Vt. ⌋	Vermont.	
V. P. \ l.	Vice President.	
W. I. (⁄	West Indies.	
Wm. ℰ	William.	
W. T. (—	Washington Territory.	
Zach. ⌣	Zachariah.	

DIRECTIONS.

E.	⌣.	East.
W.	(	West.
N.	).	North.
S.	⌣·	South.
E S. E.	⌣ . ⌣ . ⌣	East Southeast.
N. W.	) (	Northwest.
S. E.	⌣ · ⌣	Southeast.
S. S. E.	⌣ . ⌣ . ⌣	South Southeast.
S. W.	⌣ . (	Southwest.
N. N. W.	) .) . (	North Northwest.
W. S. W.	(. ⌣ . (	West Southwest.

DAYS OF WEEK.

Mon.	⌒	Fri.	✓
Tues.	⌒	Sat.	⌣
Wednes.	⌒	Sun.	⌣
Thurs.	⌒		

MONTHS.

Jan.	⌒	July.	⌒
Feb.	⌐	Aug.	𝟸
Mar.	𝟪	Sept.	⌒
Apr.	𝒱	Oct.	𝓛
May.	⌠	Nov.	𝟚
Ju.	?	Dec.	⌒

READING EXERCISE XXIV.

Speech of Patrick Henry.

[Shorthand content]

WRITING EXERCISE XXIV.

Speech of Patrick Henry.

MR. PRESIDENT: It is natural to man to indulge in the illusion of hope. We are apt to shut our eyes against a painful truth —and listen to the song of that syren, till she transforms us into beasts. Is this the part of wise men, engaged in a great and arduous struggle for liberty? Are we disposed to be of the number of those, who having eyes, see not, and having ears, hear not the things which so nearly concern their temporal salvation? For my part, whatever anguish of spirit it may cost, I am willing to know the truth; to know the worst and to provide for it.

I have but one lamp by which my feet are guided; and that is the lamp of experience. I know no way of judging of the future but by the past, and judging by the past, I wish to know what there has been in the conduct of the British ministry, for the last ten years, to justify those hopes with which these gentlemen have been pleased to solace themselves and the House? Is it that insidious smile with which our petition has been lately received? Trust it not, it will prove a snare to your feet. Suffer not yourself to be betrayed with a kiss. Ask yourselves how this gracious reception of our petition comports with those warlike preparations which cover our waters and darken our land. Are fleets and armies necessary to a work of love and reconciliation? Have we

Speech of Patrick Henry.

Speech of Patrick Henry.

shown ourselves so unwilling to be reconciled, that force must be called in to win back our love? Let us not deceive ourselves, sir. These are the implements of war and subjection—the last argument to which kings resort. I ask these gentlemen, sir, what means this martial array, if its purpose be not to force us to submission? Can they assign any other possible motive for it? Has Great Britain any enemy in this quarter of the world, to call for all this accumulation of warriors and armies? No, sir, she has none. They are meant for us; they can be meant for no other. They are sent over to bind and rivet upon us those chains, which the British ministry have been so long forging. And what have we to oppose to them? Shall we try argument? Sir, we have been trying that for the last ten years. Have we any thing new to offer on the subject? Nothing. We have held the subject up in every light of which it is capable; but it has been all in vain. Shall we resort to entreaty and humble supplication? What terms shall we find, which have not been already exhausted?

Let us not, I beseech you, sir, deceive ourselves longer. We have done everything that could be done, to avert the storm which is now coming on. We have petitioned; we have remonstrated; we have supplicated; we have prostrated ourselves before the throne, and have implored its interposition to arrest the tyrannical hands of the ministry and parliament. Our petitions have been

Speech of Patrick Henry.

Speech of Patrick Henry.

slighted; our remonstrances have produced additional violence and insult; our supplications have been disregarded; and we have been spurned with contempt, from the foot of the throne. In vain, after these things, may we indulge in the fond hope of peace and reconciliation. There is no longer any room for hope. If we wish to be free—if we mean to preserve inviolate those inestimable privileges for which we have been so long contending—if we mean not falsely to abandon the noble struggle in which we have been so long engaged, and which we have pledged ourselves never to abandon, until the glorious object of our contest shall be obtained—we must fight—I repeat it sir, we must fight!! An appeal to arms and to the God of Hosts is all that is left us!

They tell us, sir, that we are weak—unable to cope with so formidable an adversary. But when shall we be stronger? Will it be the next week, or the next year? Will it be when we are totally disarmed, and when a British guard shall be stationed in every house? Shall we gather strength by irresolution and inaction? Shall we acquire the means of effectual resistance by lying supinely on our backs and hugging the delusive phantom of hope, until our enemies have bound us hand and foot? Sir, we are not weak, if we make a proper use of those means which the God of nature hath placed in our power. Three millions of people, armed in the holy cause of liberty, and in such a country

SPEECH OF PATRICK HENRY.

Speech of Patrick Henry.

as we possess, are invincible by any force which our enemy can send against us. Besides, sir, we shall not fight our battles alone. There is a just God, who presides over the destinies of nations, and who will raise up friends to fight our battles for us. The battle, sir, is not to the strong alone; it is to the vigilant, the active, the brave. Besides, sir, we have no election. If we were base enough to desire it, it is now too late to retire from the contest. There is no retreat, but in submission and slavery! Our chains are forged. Their clanking may be heard on the plains of Boston! The war is inevitable—and let it come!! I repeat it, sir, let it come!! It is in vain, sir, to extenuate the matter. These gentlemen may cry peace, peace—but there is no peace. The war is actually begun. The next gale that sweeps from the north will bring to our ears the clash of resounding arms! Our brethren are already in the field! Why stand we here idle? What is it that these gentlemen wish? What would they have? Is life so dear, or peace so sweet as to be purchased at the price of chains and slavery? Forbid it, Almighty God! I know not what course others may take, but as for me, GIVE ME LIBERTY OR GIVE ME DEATH.

READING EXERCISE XXV.
A Centennial Address.

WRITING EXERCISE XXV.

A Centennial Address.

When we reflect on what has been, and what is now, is it possible not to feel a profound sense of the responsibleness of this Republic to all future ages? What vast motives press upon us for lofty effort! What brilliant prospects invite our enthusiasm! What solemn warnings at once demand our vigilance and moderate our confidence! The old world has already revealed to us in its unsealed books, the beginning and end of all of its own marvelous struggles in the cause of liberty. Greece, lovely Greece, "the land of scholars and the nurse of arms," where sister republics in fair processions chanted the praises of liberty and the gods; where and what is she? For two thousand years her oppressor has bound her to the earth. Her arts are no more. The last sad relics of her temples are but the barracks for a ruthless soldiery; the fragments of her churches and palaces are in the dust, yet beautiful in ruin. She fell not when the mighty were upon her. Her sons were united at Thermopylæ and Marathon; and the tide of her triumphs rolled back upon the Hellespont. She was conquered by her own factions. She fell by the hands of her own people. The man of Macedonia did not the work of destruction. It was already done by her own corruptions, banishments and dissensions.

Rome, republican Rome, whose eagles glanced in the rising and setting sun; where, and what is she? The eternal city yet remains, proud even in her desolation, noble in her decline, ven-

A Centennial Address.

A CENTENNIAL ADDRESS.

erable in the majesty of religion, and calm as in the composure of death. More than eighteen centuries have mourned over the loss of her empire. A mortal disease was upon her vitals before Cæsar had crossed the Rubicon; and Brutus did not restore her health by the deep probings of the Senate chamber. The Goths, and Vandals and Huns, the swarms of the north, completed only what was already begun at home. The legions were bought and sold, but the people offered the tribute money.

And where are the republics of modern times, which clustered around immortal Italy? Venice and Genoa exist but in name. The Alps, indeed, look down upon the brave and peaceful Swiss in their native fastness, but their guaranty of their freedom is in their weakness, and not in their strength. The mountains are not easily crossed, and the valleys are not easily retained. When the invader comes, he moves like an avalanche, carrying destruction in his path. The peasantry sinks before him. The country is too poor for plunder and too rough for valuable conquest. Nature presents her eternal barriers on every side to check the wantonness of ambition; and Switzerland remains with her simple institutions, a military road to fairer climates, scarcely worth a permanent possession, and protected by the jealousy of her neighbors.

We stand the latest, and if we fail, probably the last experiment of self-government by the people We have begun it under circumstances of the most auspicious nature. We are in the vigor of youth. Our growth has never been checked by the

A Centennial Address.

A Centennial Address.

oppressions of tyranny. Our constitutions have never been enfeebled by the vices or luxuries of the old world. Such as we are, we have been from the beginning; simple, hardy, intelligent, accustomed to self-government and self-respect.

The Atlantic rolls between us and any formidable foe. Within our own territory, stretching through many degrees of latitude and longitude, we have the choice of many products, and many means of independence. The government is mild. The press is free. Religion is free. Knowledge reaches, or may reach every home. What fairer prospects of success could be presented? What means more adequate to accomplish the sublime end? What more is neccessary than for the people to preserve what they themselves have created? Already has the age caught the spirit of our institutions. It has already ascended the Andes and snuffed the breezes of both oceans. It has infused itself into the life-blood of Europe, and warmed the sunny plains of France, and the low-lands of Holland. It has touched the philosophy of Germany in the north and, moving onward to the south, has opened to Greece the lessons of her better days.

Can it be that America under such circumstances, can betray the inspiration of whose ruin is, "they were, but they are not." Forbid it, my countrymen, forbid it, heaven! I call upon you, fathers, by the shades of your ancestors, by the dear ashes which repose in this precious soil, by all you are, and all you expect to be, to resist every project of disunion, every encroachment upon your liberties.

A Centennial Address.

A Centennial Address.

I call upon you, mothers, by that which never fails in woman, the love of your off-spring; teach them as they climb your knees or lean upon your bosom, the blessings of liberty. Swear them at the altar, as with their baptismal vows, to be true to their country, and never to forget or to forsake her.

I call upon you, young men, to remember whose sons you are, whose inheritance you possess. Life can never be too short, which brings nothing but disgrace and oppression. Death never comes too soon, if necessary in defense of the liberties of your country.

I call upon you, old men, for your counsel, and your prayers, and your benedictions. May not your gray hairs go down in sorrow to the grave, with the recollection that you have lived in vain. May not your last sun sink in the west on a nation of slaves.

No — I read in the destiny of my country far better hopes, far brighter visions. We, who are now assembled here, must soon be gathered to the congregation of other days. The time for our departure is at hand, to make way for our children upon the theatre of life. May God speed them and theirs. May he who at the distance of another century shall stand here to celebrate this day, still look around upon a free, happy and virtuous people. May he have reason to exult as we do. May he, with all the enthusiasm of truth, as well as poetry, exclaim, that here is still his country.

Zealous yet modest; innocent, though free;
Patient of toil; serene amidst alarms;
Inflexible in faith; invincible in arms.

PERNIN'S PRACTICAL REPORTER.

READING EXERCISE XXVI.

Portion of Testimony given in a Patent Case.

WRITING EXERCISE XXVI.

PORTION OF TESTIMONY GIVEN IN A PATENT CASE.

NORTHERN DISTRICT OF NEW YORK, }
    COUNTY OF SENECA. } ss.

Depositions taken at Seneca Falls, Seneca County, in said district, on the 9th of August, 1870, at Hoag's Hotel.

Present, W. W. Leggett, of counsel for complainants.
    "   E. W. Paige,   "   defendants.

Mr. E. W. Paige, on part of defendants, introduced by consent of counsel for complainants, the testimony of Jacob Bachman, from the printed Ohio records, in the case of JOHN C. BIRDSALL, *against* ANGUS MCDONALD, AND OTHERS, pages 246 to 250 inclusive.

Jacob Bachman, being duly sworn, says:

1st Ques. Are you the same Jacob Bachman whose deposition has just been read?

Ans. Yes sir.

2d Ques. In your answer to question eleven in that deposition you stated that you saw Mr. Feazler operating his combined machine at Mr. Hoster's barn in Fayette, and you thought it was in 1857. Can you now fix that date exactly?

Ans. To the best of my knowledge it was in 1856.

3d Ques. At what time in the year of 1856?

Ans. I think in December.

4th Ques. State how you know it was in 1856?

Ans. I moved from Clifton Springs back to Fayette in the Fall

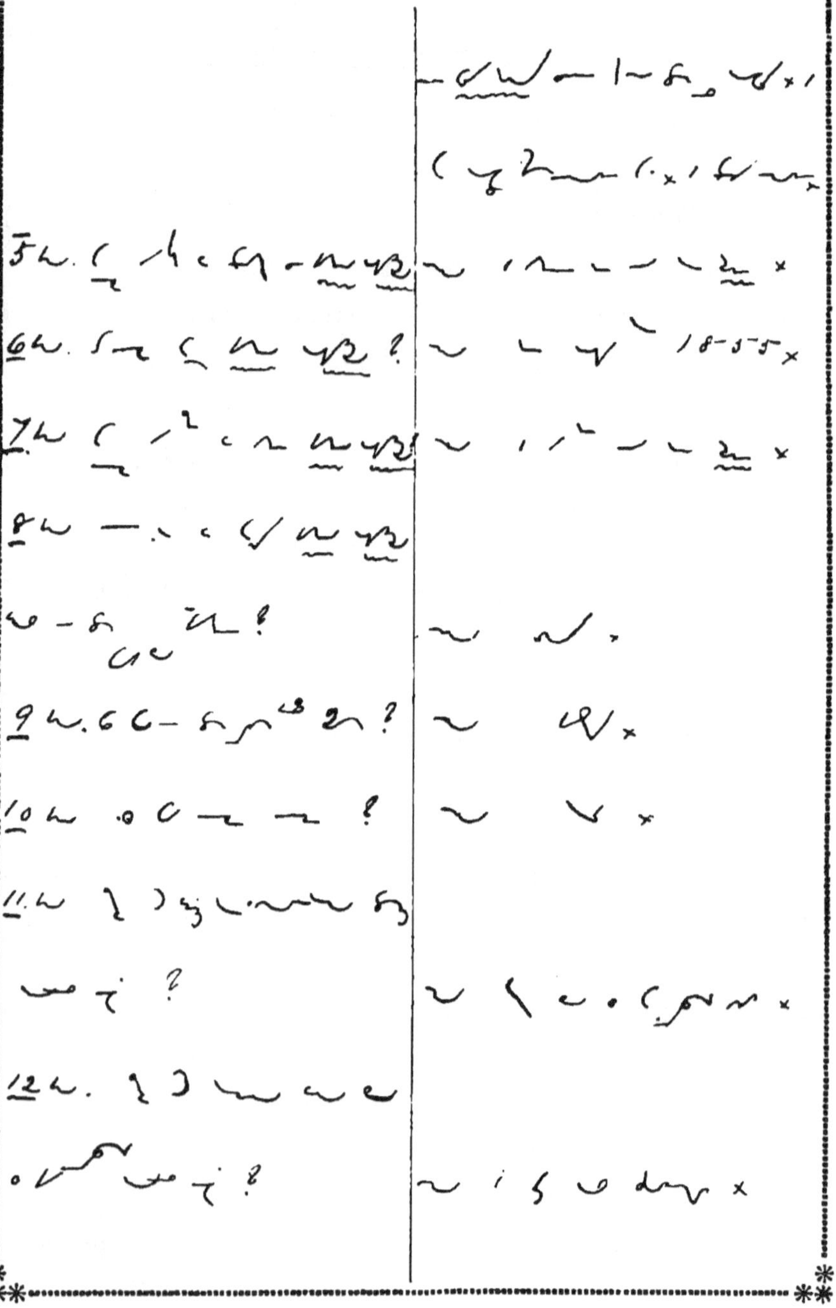

of 1856, and Mr. Freazler had built his machine that summer. I was somewhat anxious to see it work. I went there to see it.

5th Ques. Where did you live before you went to live at Clifton Springs?

Ans. I lived in the town of Fayette.

6th Ques. When did you move to Clifton Springs?

Ans. In the spring of 1855.

7th Ques. Where did you live after you left Clifton Springs ?

Ans. I lived in the town of Fayette.

8th Ques. And when you moved from Clifton Springs you saw the machine working as described?

Ans. Yes, sir.

9th Ques. What was the machine threshing on that occasion?

Ans. Clover.

10th Ques. How well did it do it?

Ans. Very well.

11th Ques. Have you known anything of the history of this machine since that time?

Ans. I have as a wheat thresher only.

12th Ques. Have you known of its use as a clover thresher since that time?

Ans. I couldn't say, positively.

13th Ques. Have you known of its use among the farmers about as a clover thresher since that time?

Ans. By hearsay only.

Cross-examination by counsel for complainants.

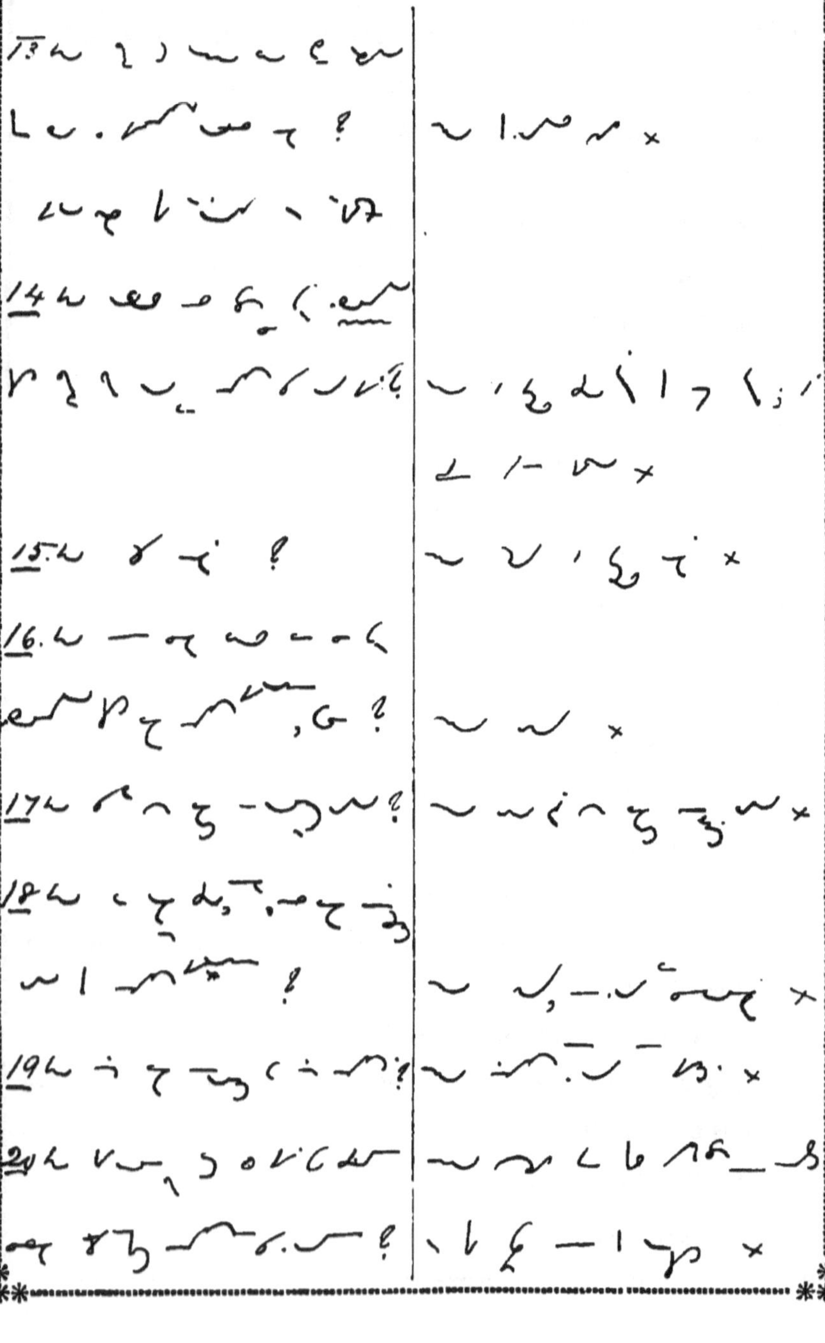

14th Ques. Since you say you saw that machine at work in Hoster's barn, have you ever seen it thresh or hull clover?

Ans. I could not say positively I have, but think I have; I cannot give the place.

15th Ques. Nor the time?

Ans. No, sir, I couldn't say the time.

16th Ques. And at the time you saw it at work in Hoster's barn it was threshing clover seed, was it?

Ans. Yes, sir.

17th Ques. Are you sure it was not doing something else?

Ans. Yes, I am sure it was not doing anything else.

18th Ques. You swear positively, then, do you, that it was doing nothing else but threshing clover seed?

Ans. Yes, sir, and hulling it at the same time.

19th Ques. Then it was doing something more than threshing?

Ans. Threshing and hulling and cleaning.

20th Ques. Please state if you know how clover was gathered at that time preparatory to being threshed or hulled.

Ans. Generally cut by a reaper machine, and drawn in by wagon and put into barn.

21st Ques. When you gave your testimony in the *Ohio cases*, who asked you to give your testimony?

Ans. Mr. Corwin, here in town, came up after me.

22d Ques. Did Mr. George Westinghouse call upon you for

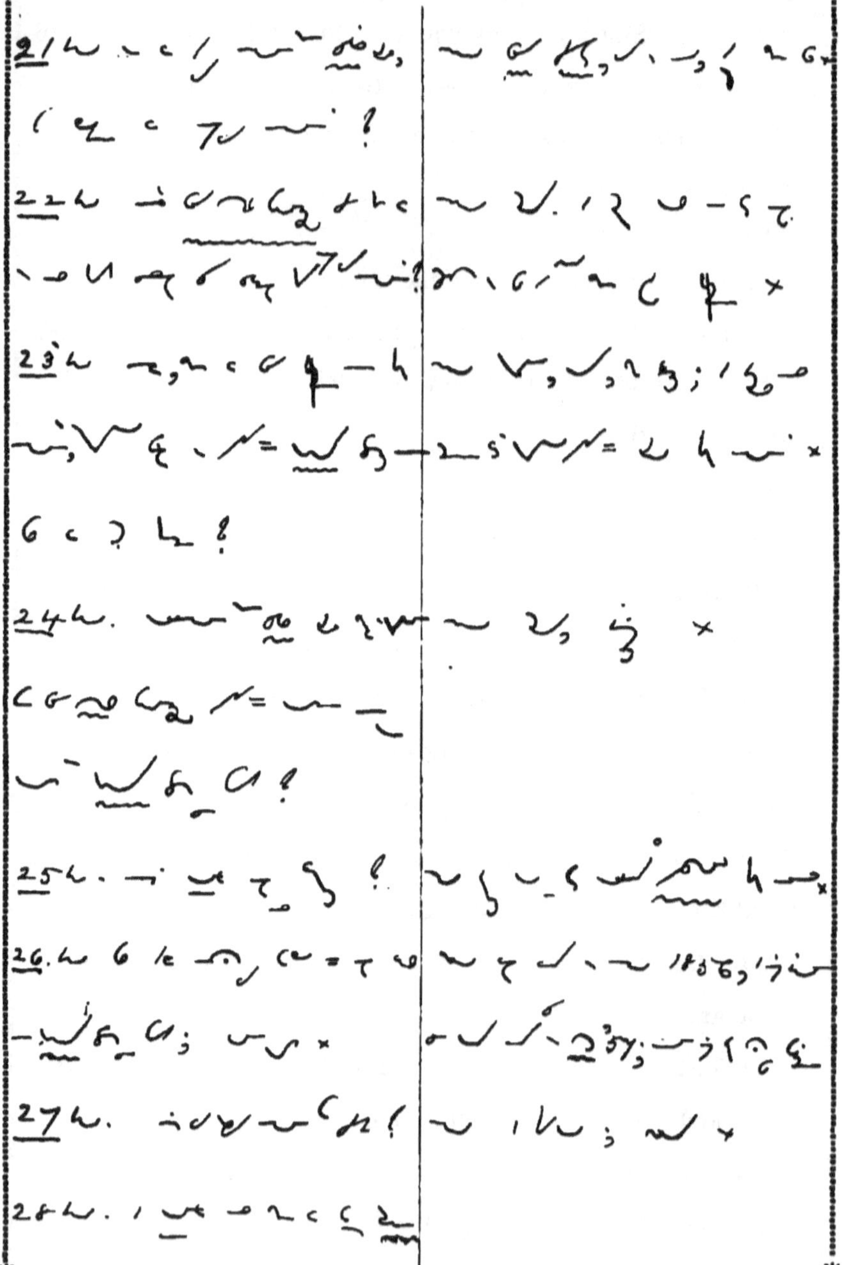

that purpose at that time or at any time prior to giving your testimony?

Ans. No, sir, I never saw the man to my knowledge in my life, until after I was subpœned.

23*d Ques.* Did you, after you were subpœned and before testifying, converse with him in relation to the Feazler machine and what you knew about it?

Ans. Very little, sir, if anything; I couldn't say that we had any conversation relative to the case before testifying.

24*th Ques.* Since testifying in the *Ohio cases* have you conversed with Mr. George Westinghouse relative to the said date of seeing the Feazler machine at work?

Ans. No, sir, I think not.

25*th Ques.* Do I understand you to mean that you have not?

Ans. I have not seen the man since the trial at Rochester, before to-day.

26*th Ques.* What caused you to change your mind as to the time you saw the Feazler machine at work; state fully.

Ans. It was either in *December*, 1856, I think I said at the other trial, or in *January*, 1857; I don't think I have changed my mind as to the date.

27*th Ques.* Then your former testimony was correct?

Ans. I believe so; yes, sir.

28*th Ques.* I understand you that after you moved to Fayette, you saw the Feazler machine at work in Hoster's barn; about how

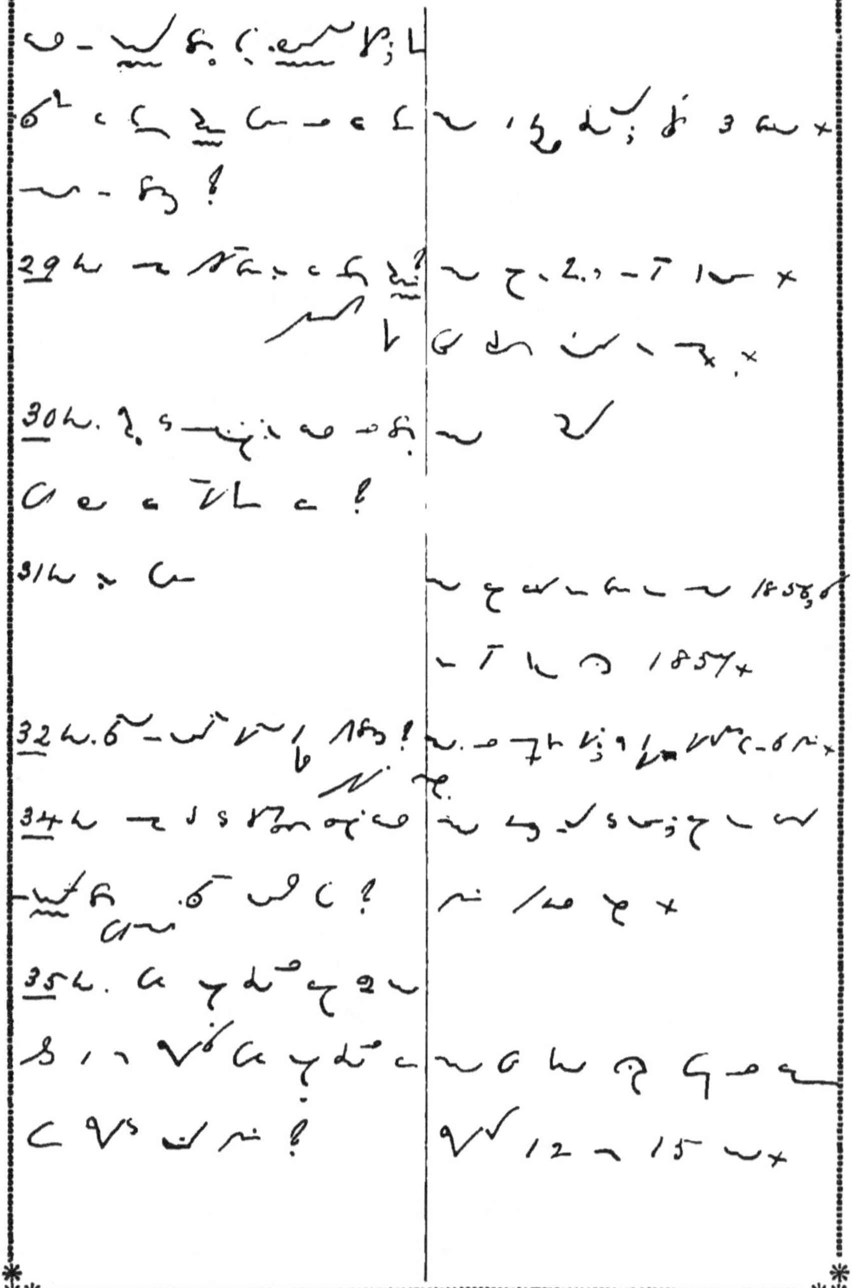

118 — PERNIN'S PRACTICAL REPORTER.

(shorthand content — not transcribable)

long after you moved to Fayette was it that you went to see the machine?

Ans. I couldn't say positively, sir; probably three months.

29*th Ques.* Do you recollect the month when you went to Fayette?

Ans. It was in October, the first part of it.

Re-direct by Mr. Page, counsel for defendants.

30*th Ques.* Have you now any doubt of the time when you saw that machine work as you described it?

Ans. No, sir.

31*st Ques.* When was it?

Ans. It was either in the month of December, 1856, or in the first part of 1857, in January.

32*d Ques.* How long is the straw when clover is cut by a reaper machine?

Ans. That depends upon clover; if cut close to ground, pretty much the whole length of the clover.

Re-cross-examination.

34*th Ques.* Did you pay particular attention at the time you saw the Feazler machine working to see how long the straw was?

Ans. I did not measure any of it, it was of the usual length raised on that farm.

35*th Ques.* Will you say positively that it was two inches long on an average, or will you swear positively that it would average any other length?

Ans. My best judgment would be that it would average from twelve to fifteen inches.

READING EXERCISE XXVII.

Counsel to the Young. (See p. 45, Instructor.)

WHAT PROMINENT NEWSPAPERS SAY.

The Duployan System is in common use in the schools of France, and is easy to be learned. It has the advantage over others in avoiding shading and the large number of angles, and in the use of the circles for vowels.—[Chicago Evening Journal.

Pernin's "Phonographic Instructor" has already been favorably noticed in the columns of the Free Press, and it is a gratification to note that its success has warranted the publication of the second edition, revised and enlarged. The system is an adaptation to the English language of the French or Duployc system, which is a regular study in the French schools, where children of twelve and fourteen years of age become verbatim reporters. It abbreviates very much the labor necessary in learning and using the other systems. It is certainly worthy the careful examination of all interested in Stenography, especially of those who contemplate the study thereof.—[Detroit Free Press.

The remarkable rapidity with which this system is acquired bids fair to make it very popular, not only with press reporters, but with men and women employed in any business where the pen is used.—[Essex (Ont) Times.

The Pernin method of short-hand writing is superior to other systems, and is a saving of time.—[Chicago Daily Inter-Ocean.

The Pernin "Phonographic Instructor" contains a system of short-hand writing in five lessons, adapted from the Duploye system. From careful inspection of the work we are able to say it is very complete and practical, amply explicit in instruction to beginners in the art, and will also prove beneficial to more advanced pupils.—[Chicago Post.

Pernin's Phonographic Instructor comprises a system containing *marked advantages* over all others in use. By the aid of this book the student may become a phonographer in a short time.—[Detroit Evening News.

We have been much interested in looking over Pernin's adaptation to the English of the Duployan short-hand. The system is one of great value, and is arranged with great simplicity. It seems to be eminently a system of sound-writing, and the characters used are carefully adapted to the greatest degree of expedition with the least degree of fatigue.—[Saturday Evening Herald, Chicago.

This system of short-hand has been adapted to the English language from Duploye's French System, which has become so popular in France and the continent of Europe as to be adopted as a general study in the public schools, and so simple and easily acquired that children of twelve and fourteen years of age are capable of verbatim reporting. In our age of rapid work and thought, a more simple and rapid system of writing is greatly to be desired. The different methods of short-hand now in use require so much time and application to make them practical, that but few can afford the time to possess the art; but this system of using similar signs for a number of sounds, and the simplest and least number of characters possible, so as to avoid burdening the memory, is the simplest and most rapid system of phonography in use.—[Detroit Post and Tribune.

This method, by a combination of the consonants and vowels, obtains an advantage over other systems of stenography that must inevitably result in a great saving of time to the reporter. The fewest possible phonographs are used consistent with legibility. The student, in a few weeks, may undoubtedly acquire a knowledge of the system.—[Chicago Times.

At this day of telephoning, phonographing and telegraphing by sound, the various short-hand systems are undergoing examination such as they have never received, with a view of testing their relative merits and applicability to the enormous strides which invention has been making. The present system certainly surpasses in practicability any now in use, and we feel assured, from a careful comparison of all the leading methods of phonography, that none compares with the French in simplicity, legibility and adaptability to the wants of all professional men and the phonography of all languages.—[The Conservative, Salem, Va.

Extracts of a few Letters from Writers of the System.

Duployé's Stenography, adapted to the English, is really the simplest and easiest of all systems in use.—[Rev. J. T. Wagner, Windsor, Ont.

The more I use your system the more I am satisfied of its superiority over any with which I am acquainted.—[E. C. Bittle, M.A., Roanoke College, Salem, Va.

Some three weeks ago my brother, Col. B. Mason, placed in my hands your "Phonographic Instructor." By this you will see what progress I have already made with no teacher but the book. The system is so simple that I feel confident of being able to write with rapidity by a moderate practice of two or three months.—[Thomas Mason, Yonkers, N.Y.

I have used some of my spare hours in the study of your book, with results gratifying to myself, at least. This will show the result of my unassisted study since I received your book. Such progress in so short a time speaks well for the system. I am greatly pleased.—[Wm. Aug. Gibson, Yonkers, N. Y.

During the last six months I have reported five hundred lectures and copied them ready for publication. With the old methods this would have been almost an impossibility, owing to the confinement, fatigue and attention which would be required to perform such a work.—[R. H. Stevens, Medical Dept. Mich. University, Ann Arbor.

I have studied and had some experience in teaching Duployé's System with Pernin's English adaptation, and am much pleased with it. I find it very simple, very easily acquired, and yet very complete. My classes are invariably pleased with it.—[W. F. Jewell, Goldsmith's Business University, Detroit, Mich.

I have studied your work on Phonography. For the benefit of education it should be taught in all our schools and colleges, and I think it our duty to propagate it as much as it is in our power.—[Prof. A. Mainville, St. Viateur's College, Bourbonnais Grove, Kankakee Co., Ill.

About one year ago a copy of your instruction book on Duploye's Phonography fell into my hands. A brief examination convinced me of the *unrivalled merits* of Duploye's system. I have since taught about a hundred pupils to read and write by your method. My pupils have been of ages from eight years to sixty. Without an exception they have learned rapidly, and have become active agents in recommending the system to others. The more I write it, the more I am astonished at its wonderful simplicity and its surprising legibility. —[Col. B. Mason, Pres. Yonkers Military Institute, Yonkers, N. Y.

I can say of your system of Phonography that I have derived more pleasure and profit from two months' study of it than from one year's study of Graham's hand-book of standard phonography. It contains no abstract word-sign to burden the memory. Everything is a logical gradation from the first page of the "Instructor" to the last page of the "Treatise of Abbreviations."—[D. Hall, Principal School, Caseville, Huron Co., Mich.

I feel that I have made excellent progress in your System of Stenography. I started a while after two Graham students, who are taking instructions from the official court stenographer here, and with the little instruction received by mail I am far in advance of them, and am now reporting for one of our papers. I, at one time, studied the Munson system faithfully, but did not know much more when I left off than when I commenced—at least, could not read half what I had written a short time afterward. I think the Duployan is *"the"* system for anyone to adopt, unless he wishes to devote a lifetime to acquiring the art. —[Arthur Nicholas, W. Federal St., Youngstown, Ohio.

I am employed as stenographer in the general offices here of the Wabash, St. Louis & P. R'y, and experience no difficulty in either writing or reading your system. I am now fully convinced that I made a very profitable investment when I concluded to take lessons from you. My friends will scarcely believe me when I tell them that I was fitted for my position in four months, and it is hardly to be wondered at when one considers the length of time it takes to acquire any of the other systems of short-hand now in use. If the Duployan system were only extensively advertised, and the general public made aware of how easily it is learned and how rapid and legible it is, very few would care to adopt the other systems which, with their word-signs, shaded lines, etc., burden the memory so greatly, and after years spent in acquiring them, they are then no better, nor as good, as the Duployan. I shall always be most happy to give your system that recommendation that I feel sure it merits.—[J. F. Barron, Sten. Wabash Gen'l Office, Detroit, Mich.

We, the undersigned members of last winter's class of Stenography, are pleased to state that we think the Duployan System superior to and more easily attained than any other short-hand method now in use, and can highly recommend it to all intending learners.—[Charles E. Ovenshire, W. Seymour McIntosh, Wm. J. Moore, with Throp, Hawley & Co., 85–87 Jefferson avenue, Detroit.

It is with pleasure that I write to inform you of my progress in Stenography. It is but a trifle more than four months since I first saw your system, and I can now easily take *in full* the discourses of the most rapid speakers among our corps of lecturers. At the end of the first month, putting less than two hours' work to it per day, not only had I mastered the principles of both corresponding and reporting styles, but could apply those principles at the rate of thirty-five words per minute, and I have no hesitancy in asserting that any one of ordinary ability can, by confining his mind to it daily for two hours, be able at the end of three months to do as I am now doing. Not the least among the superiorities of your system over all others which I have investigated is the facility of reading it. I take pleasure in recommending it to the public for its simplicity, the ease with which it is learned and read, and its great practicability to all who have need of a rapid and legible system of writing.—[Very truly yours, W. LeRoy Crissman, Law Dept. Michigan University, Ann Arbor.

Please send me by return of post a copy of your "Practical Reporter." I have taught the system from your "Phonographic Instructor" to several gentlemen here, who are all delighted with its simplicity. I should like to be appointed agent for the sale of your books here.—[Yours truly, John M. Sloan, 20 N. Frederick Street, Dublin, Ireland.

PERNIN'S
Phonographic Institute.

INSTRUCTION PRIVATELY OR IN CLASSES.

TERMS:

Corresponding Course,	$15 00
Reporting Course,	15 00
Complete Course,	30 00
Tuition by Month,	10 00
Single Lessons,	1 00
Lessons by Mail, Exclusive of Postage, each,	50

Reduction to Classes.

PERNIN'S PHONOGRAPHIC PUBLICATIONS.

Phonographic Instructor (3d edition), Paper,	$ 50
" " " Cloth,	1 00
Pernin's Practical Reporter, Cloth,	1 50

Liberal Discount to Schools and Colleges.

For Books or Instruction, address,

H. M. PERNIN,

68 Farrar St., **DETROIT, MICH.**
Near Public Library,

www.ingramcontent.com/pod-product-compliance
Lightning Source LLC
Chambersburg PA
CBHW020118170426
43199CB00009B/559